What educators are saying about...
Snail Trails

"This book provides a starting place for the educator of young children. It reveals how skilled teachers handle children's reactions to natural materials brought into the classroom, and is a good example of how to help them construct the world around them."

from the Foreword by
Roger Tory Peterson
Roger Tory Peterson Institute of Natural History

"...the step-by-step account of Sue and Beth's classroom learning experiences with animal visitors and preschool children is reassuring, understandable and invitational."

Helen Ross Russell, Author
*10 Minute Field Trips Using
the School Grounds to Teach*
and Environmental Science Consultant

"This is a delightful and stimulating science program for young children. It's easy enough for the teacher with a limited science background or no science experience. It can also serve as a starting point for more experienced teachers."

Billie Jean Gerren
Demonstration Teacher
Seeds University
Elementary School, UCLA

Roger Tory Peterson Institute of Natural History

Pacific Oaks College and Children's Programs

Snail Trails and Tadpole Tails

Nature Education Guide for Young Children

by
Richard Cohen
and
Betty Phillips Tunick

Illustrator Kurt Seaberg

Based on the classrooms of
Beth Reeves-Fortney
and
Sue Bush

Redleaf Press
a division of Resources for Child Caring

Dedication

To Beth and Sue for allowing us into their classrooms and their minds, and for helping us see the joy of children learning about nature.

Published by: Redleaf Press
                 a division of Resources for Child Caring
                 450 North Syndicate, Suite 5
                 St. Paul, Minnesota 55104

Distributed by: Gryphon House
                 P.O. Box 275
                 Mt. Rainier, Maryland 20712

ISBN: 0-934140-78-2

Library of Congress Cataloging-in-Publication Data

Cohen, Richard, 1951-
     Snail trails and tadpole tails : nature education for young
children / Richard Cohen & Betty Phillips Tunick ; foreword by Roger
Tory Peterson.
          p.   cm.
     "With the support of the Roger Tory Peterson Institute of Natural
History (and) Pacific Oaks College and Children's Programs."
     Includes bibliographical references and index.
     ISBN 0-934140-78-2 (pbk.) : $12.95
     1. Nature study—United States.   2. Education, Preschool—Activity
programs—United States.   3. Natural history—Study and teaching—
United States.   4. Interdisciplinary approach in education—United
States.   I. Tunick, Betty Phillips.   II. Roger Tory Peterson
Institute.   III. Pacific Oaks College.   IV. Title.
LB1140.5.S35C64   1993
372.3'57—dc20   93-5850
                                                   CIP

Printed in the United States of America.

Acknowledgments

The contributions of many people and organizations made this guide a reality. All deserve more thanks than we can squeeze into an acknowledgments page.

Dr. Kathryn Girard, Director of Research, Development, and Computing at Pacific Oaks, and Dr. William Sharp, Director of Education at the Roger Tory Peterson Institute of Natural History, developed the initial idea for this guide and encouraged our progress.

Thank you to Jeff Hohensee and Linda Slater who did research and Anne Schiller who sifted through mounds of materials and an orgy of organizations to find and evaluate resources. Anne also organized the review of the manuscript. Thank you to Judy Kantor and Jean Miyamato of the library at Seeds University Elementary School, and the laboratory school of the UCLA Graduate School of Education, who found the fiction and poetry resources. Thank you to Holly Cannon, Assistant to the Director of the Pacific Oaks Research Center, who painstakingly formatted and copy-edited the many pieces into a unified manuscript. Susan Fong, at the California Community Foundation, was supportive and patient despite many delays.

We appreciated the help of Betty Jones in developing the focus and big ideas for this project. The chapter on snails is based on the work of Linda Morris. We thank her for her assistance.

We would also like to thank the following people for reviewing the manuscript and for their suggestions and comments: Elizabeth and Elisha Atkins, MD; Jennifer Berke; Happie Byers; Joseph Cornell; Jane Dickson; Billie Jean Gerren; Jackie Gould; Margaret Maier; Pat McDonagh; Taka Nomura; Dr. Helen Ross Russell; and Miriam Westervelt. Any errors remaining are the authors. We would also like to thank Dr. David Sobel for his invaluable help in locating nature references.

Finally, generous financial support came from The California Community Foundation, The Roger Tory Peterson Institute of Natural History, and the State of New York.

Roger Tory Peterson Institute of Natural History
Pacific Oaks College and Children's Programs

Nature Education Guide
for Young Children

Table of Contents

I.   **Foreword** 8

II.   **Introduction** 9
     How to Use this Guide

III. **A Guide to the Guide** 10
    A. What Do We Mean by "Nature Education"? 10
    B. Why Is Nature Education Important? 10
    C. How Children Learn 10
    D. Why Mini-Habitats?` 11
    E. The Role of the Teacher 11, 12
    F. The Role of the Environment 13
    G. Goals 13, 14
        1. Connections with the natural world
        2. Connections with children's experiences
        3. Connections with other parts of the curriculum
    H. Working with Mixed-Age Groups 15
    I. Talking about Death 15

IV. **Stories of Five Mini-Habitats** 17
    A. Tadpoles to Frogs 19
    B. Earthworms 29
    C. Praying Mantises 43
    D. Silkworms 53
    E. Snails 63

Table of Contents

V.   Other Mini-Habitats to Try 75

    A.   Caterpillars to Butterflies 77

    B.   Ladybugs 81

    C.   Fish and Pond Environments 83

VI. Teacher Resources 87

    A.   Organizations 89, 90

    B.   Recommended Books 90

        1. Science 90, 91

        2. Early Childhood and Teaching 91

        3. Children and Community Violence 92

        4. Children and Death 92

    C.   Recommended Articles 92

Foreword
to the
Nature Education Guide for Young Children
By
Roger Tory Peterson

I can recall the exact date and time I became obsessed with birds. It was in the early morning of April 8, 1920, when a friend and I crossed the railroad tracks to explore new territory. As we entered a grove of maples near the edge of town, I spotted a brown bundle of feathers clinging to the trunk of a tree. It was a flicker, and I thought it was dead.

Very gingerly, I touched it on the back. The flicker exploded into life at my touch, with a wild look in its eye. The red marking on the back of its head showed and, in a flash of bright yellow wings, it flew away.

It was that explosion that did it. What seemed like an inert, dead thing was very much alive. It was like a resurrection, an affirmation of life. Ever since then, birds have seemed to me to be the most vivid expression of life. The natural world became my real world.

Today with our concern for environmental literacy, I believe that young children do not start with ecological concepts. They acquire them by using specific springboards such as experiences with birds, plants and other aspects of nature. To expect youngsters to become instant ecologists is presumptuous. In teaching children about the natural world, I think feelings must come first, then come the names of things, then what they do and where they live. The concepts follow the passion.

This basic philosophy underlies the programs developed by the Roger Tory Peterson Institute of Natural History. Our mission is to inform society about the natural world through the study and teaching of natural history. In keeping with this, it is our goal to create a passion for the knowledge of the natural world in the hearts and minds of children.

Snail Trails and Tadpole Tails is a result of a collaboration between Pacific Oaks College and the Roger Tory Peterson Institute. It reflects the fact that naturalists and early childhood educators share a common commitment to exploring the wholeness of our respective interests.

This book provides a starting place for the educator of young children. It reveals how skilled teachers handle children's reactions to natural materials brought into the classroom, and is a good example of how to help them construct the world around them. The suggested activities all lead to outdoor experiences in the school yard or at a local natural area. I believe that such early experiences will help lay the foundation for igniting a passion for nature in the next generation.

Introduction

How to Use this Guide

Welcome to the *Guide to Nature Education* developed by the Roger Tory Peterson Institute of Natural History and Pacific Oaks College.

If you've never done nature activities with your children before, or if you've never felt comfortable about what you do, you're in the right place. On the other hand, if you're an experienced teacher and want to learn how to develop new nature activities and integrate them into your curriculum, you're in the right place, too.

Our guide is based on the stories of what two wonderful teachers—Sue Bush and Beth Reeves-Fortney—did with their respective groups of three- and four-year-olds. What they did was to create what we call "mini-habitats" and then build many activities in and out of their classrooms around them. Through the stories, you will be able to see children's day-by-day experiences as they explore the mini-habitats. And most importantly, you'll be able to see how Sue and Beth respond to the discoveries.

Mini-habitats sound fancy. But as you'll see, they are really simple, inexpensive ways to bring parts of the natural environment into your classroom.

You can use this guide in a number of ways. Each chapter begins with a description of the habitat, an explanation of how to set it up, and a list of the activities Sue or Beth prepared to accompany it. You can simply prepare those habitats and do those activities.

But you can do more than that. Sue and Beth have a strong understanding of how children learn and of how to present nature. They are also keen observers of children. The activities they developed emerged as they watched their children's responses to the mini-habitats. The reason these are described as stories instead of as curriculum as in other guides is so you can get an idea of how things developed and how Sue and Beth thought about what they did. Through the stories, you will be able to see children's day-to-day experiences as they explore the mini-habitats. And most importantly, you'll be able to see how Sue and Beth respond to the discoveries.

You can begin to think about nature and children this way, too. Then, as you get bolder, there are examples of other mini-habitats you can develop so you can try out this way of thinking and teaching.

In "A Guide to the Guide," we included short sections about the principles that underlie Sue and Beth's teaching. The sections provide more insight and direction about striking out on your own. At the end of each chapter, we included a list of reference materials. Finally, there is a section at the end of the book on resources—people, places, and books—that are available at low cost.

As you can see, our goal is not just to give you activities to do. Instead, we want to help you understand how these activities were developed and chosen so you can develop a nature education program that is exciting and meaningful for your children and that sets them on their way to knowing about and loving the natural world.

Richard Cohen
Betty Phillips Tunick
Fall, 1993

A Guide to the Guide

What Do We Mean by "Nature Education"?

Our idea of nature education is broad: We want children to be connected with the natural world, to be both excited by and knowledgable about it. These connections are both cognitive and emotional. They are made inside and outside your classroom and on field trips.

To know something well, to come to love it, takes careful study over a period of time. In most early childhood situations today, that kind of time is most likely to be available inside. That's why we've designed these activities to take slices of nature inside where children can study them. However, the key to the success of these activities is to reconnect them with the natural world and with other parts of children's lives.

Why Is Nature Education Important?

Nature education is important for its own sake. The natural world has inspired awe and wonder in human beings for more generations than we can count. Yet children today, especially urban children, are increasingly divorced from or frightened by this wonder, unaware of its power and beauty.

Second, in a world increasingly threatened by the effects of human behavior, we need a custodial generation of young people committed to finding solutions to ecological problems.

Third, nature is a wonderful early childhood curriculum area. The natural world is patterned, yet ever changing. Birth, growth, and death—topics of abiding interest to young children's opening minds— are central to it. And the observation, classification, and communication skills that develop in the study of nature lead to the skills and dispositions children will need to succeed in school.

How Children Learn

This guide is based on a "constructivist" educational philosophy drawn from the work of Jean Piaget and other developmental psychologists. The underlying premise is that children are naturally curious about the world and strive to understand it.

Children construct their own understanding of the world through their experiences with it. Whether they are aware of it or not, children have theories about how their world works. They develop expectations that things will happen in certain ways. When they drop something, it falls; when they call, "Teacher," you respond.

Cognitive development happens when a child interacts with part of her environment and is surprised. Her expectations are not met, and she must put her theory to the test. As she thinks about this surprise, she must either fit the event into her theory of how the world works or adjust her theory.

If the environment is sufficiently stimulating, a child's understandings develop over time as her theories about the world are tested again and again and become more and more sophisticated and interconnected.

Why Mini-Habitats?

The mini-habitat is a deceptively simple idea. At one level, it's nothing more than putting animals in simple containers with the minimum necessary materials. Then you and your children watch what happens.

But, of course, much more is going on. We have designed the mini-habitats to match the way children learn.

First, mini-habitats follow **developmentally appropriate practice.** (See the guidelines in NAEYC's *Developmentally Appropriate Practice in Early Childhood Programs Serving Children from Birth Through Age 8*. This book is listed in the Teacher Resources section.) They allow children to make choices about how to be involved; they can accommodate learners at different levels of knowledge and skill.

Second, mini-habitats are based loosely on Lilian Katz's and S. Chard's concept of **the project approach** (see page 149) to early childhood education. In this approach, learning usual academic skills is embedded in meaningful activities that go on over periods of time. Children choose how and when to be involved.

For example, there is no "reading time," but if you look through the narratives, you'll see many opportunities for children to have *literacy experiences*. They have their words written down; they use picture and reference books for information; they observe and make notes and pictures. In short, as part of their study of frogs or butterflies, they begin to simulate what literate people do. Similar things happen in other subject areas as well.

It's important to note that the goals of the project approach are broader than learning necessary skills and knowledge. Katz is also concerned about developing a generation of students who have *dispositions to be curious and to learn*. These are our goals as well. We are concerned about the "push down" of primary school techniques to younger and younger children. Through mini-habitats, children learn much information, but they maintain and develop their basic desires to learn.

Third, the development of mini-habitats over a period of weeks follows the theory of **emergent curriculum** stressed at Pacific Oaks in Pasadena, California (*Issues in Curriculum: What Resources Do Preschool Teachers Need?*). That is, the teacher, knowing her children well, carefully prepares the environment and watches how children interact with it. (See the next section for more extensive explanations on the roles of the teacher and the environment.) She then supports and facilitates their growing interest in the project as it takes unexpected directions. For example, in the "Tadpoles to Frogs" narrative, when the children feel the emerging frogs need a new home, Sue arranges a field trip to a local pond. A whole new level of connections between the children's lives and the natural world develops.

The Role of the Teacher

Your role in making this a successful experience is critical. But, surprisingly, *you don't have to be an expert in nature* for these units to go well. In fact, you can observe and learn right along with your children.

In using mini-habitats with children, you have four important roles:

preparing the environment well;

observing the children and responding to their interests;

developing local contacts and resources;

and communicating with and involving parents.

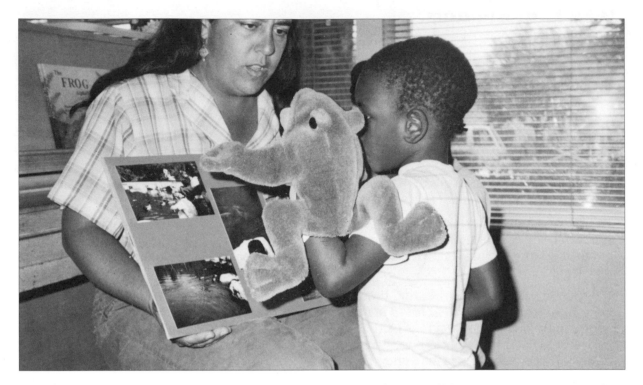

The first role of preparing the environment is so important that we will discuss it in a separate section. We should say a few words about the other roles here, though.

Observing and responding to children—No matter how many times you do these mini-habitats, the results will be different every time, and something unexpected will happen. Some of this is because different things will happen to your animals and insects. The tadpoles may be eaten by the frogs, or the earthworms may overheat and die. Children will respond to these events differently, and each year someone in your class will have a new idea.

Your job is to observe the children as they work with and observe the mini-habitats. Keep in mind the goals of the activities and respond to each new situation in a way that helps to extend and enrich what the children experience. Keep thinking of connections (see below) and ways of weaving in literacy, language, math, dramatic play, or art experiences into what is emerging.

Developing local contacts and resources—As you get more and more involved in these activities, you will find people who are interested, knowledgable, and available to help. Most communities have a nature center, and many of them have programs for young children. Local resources can also include someone at your local pet store, or a neighbor who likes to garden.

Communicating with and involving parents—Parents can be a wonderful resource in putting together a nature education program. Often, parents have skills or knowledge they can share with your class. For example, parents and grandparents often know about the animals and related lore of their cultures or native lands. We have found, however, that many parents who have grown up in cities have little experience with the natural world and its inhabitants. Help children communicate their excitement and new knowledge and engage parents in new learning as well.

Further, even if you don't have any parents with special knowledge about praying mantises or silkworms, there are other ways parents can participate. They can sit at a table and write down children's observations. They can accompany you on field trips and perhaps take photographs. They can help children turn their observations and photographs into books about the trips that can go in the class library.

The Role of the Environment

The role of the environment is to *stimulate children to engage in activities* and then to *support their sustained interest*.

The mini-habitat should be set up where a number of children can observe it easily. This will encourage them to discover it and discuss what they have found.

Once children are involved, they need near them the things that will help them have a full experience. If possible, these should include:

Magnifiers—These are available at low cost (many plastic ones cost less than a dollar apiece). They provide children with a new perspective on what they are studying. Just as importantly, they begin to learn that "doing science" involves using tools that aid observation.

Writing materials—Keep a wide variety of writing materials and papers near the mini-habitat. This encourages children's spontaneous writing and drawing of their observations. Change the kinds of paper and writing tools occasionally and see if that makes a difference. Don't be surprised if you see the beginnings of invented spelling.

Reference books, charts, etc.—Keep nonfiction materials nearby for children, teachers, and parents to refer to. Don't worry that the children may not be able to read them. As long as the pictures are clear enough, they will use them as part of their observation of the mini-habitats. It's also good for children to realize that books can be resources for important information about their world.

Goals

With mini-habitats, you don't always know what's going to happen next. You can write lesson plans about what you expect will happen, but you always have to be ready to change them when something different or more interesting arises.

We believe that the best way to be ready is to keep some goals in mind. Some of the key goals involve helping children make connections. If you plan the environment carefully, watch the children, and keep the connections below in mind, we believe you and your class will have successful and enjoyable experiences with mini-habitats.

Connections with the natural world—One of the critical parts of this curriculum is reconnecting the animals being observed to their natural environments. Sue and Beth use their yards and field trips whenever possible to let the children see how the animals live in the world outside their classrooms.

Connections with children's experience—Sue and Beth elicit and draw on children's existing knowledge and experience whenever possible. A boy in Sue's class knows that fish, not just birds, like worms as food. Connections to existing knowledge are what makes learning for young children meaningful, and one of the teacher's most important roles is to stimulate the development of those connections.

Connections with other parts of the curriculum—Notice in the narratives how many opportunities arise naturally for children to talk, write or dictate, draw or act out their experiences. All of these activities—language, writing, art, and dramatic play—are forms of representation. As children progress through school, more and more of their work will center around becoming competent in the standard ways we use to represent the world (e.g., reading and writing, numbers, the arts).

The new work on developmentally appropriate practice shows us that children acquire these skills best when they are embedded in meaningful activities rather than taught in isolation. They become so engrossed in the activities that they do not realize that they are also practicing counting, learning new vocabulary, and learning to use writing in order to record and communicate ideas and information.

Working with Mixed-Age Groups

All over the country, the move is on to bring together children with a wider range of ages. Family child care providers, of course, have known about the joys and challenges of mixed-age groups for years. Many classroom teachers are rediscovering the experience.

Developmentally appropriate practice lends itself beautifully to mixed-age groups. The idea is to provide open-ended activities that allow children to bring a wide variety of knowledge, skills, and approaches. They make the connections they are ready to make. Younger children learn by watching the older children explore. Older children, in helping those smaller, discover what teachers already know, that explaining an idea and experience helps us understand it better.

This guide is designed for use with three- and four-year-olds. We believe it would be useful for a wider range of ages as well. However, if you have infants and toddlers in your environment, put the mini-habitat somewhere less accessible to them and monitor their participation more closely. This is not so much for their benefit as to protect the animals and their containers. Adapting the mini-habitats for school-age children is easy, too. The animals themselves will be just as engaging, and the methods will be the same. Older children may need more sophisticated resource materials.

Talking about Death

Nature education is a life-affirming undertaking. We would never bring live things into the classroom so children can experience death. However, most of the animals we use in mini-habitats have relatively short life spans. And, despite our best efforts, the unexpected does happen, and sometimes animals die because of the way we have handled or cared for them.

Often our impulse in working with young children is to protect them from some of life's harsh realities. We know some teachers who remove dead animals when children are not around and then hope the children will not notice.

We believe avoiding the issue makes death even more mysterious. When animals die in your class, children should know about it and have the opportunity to discuss it. Follow their lead; answer their questions. Don't make more of death than children want to discuss, but don't ignore their interest or fears, either.

Discussing and confronting the issue is especially important in areas where death and violence affect children's everyday lives. For children who have witnessed real-life violence, the death of an animal they have observed and cared for can be particularly upsetting. It is important that you create safe opportunities for these children to talk about, draw, and act out their feelings and experiences. (We have listed some references in the Teacher Resources section that may be helpful to you in talking about death and violence with children.)

Stories of
Five Mini-Habitats

Tadpoles to Frogs

INTRODUCTION

One of the most exciting nature studies in Sue Bush's class came in the form of a habitat for would-be frogs. It takes several weeks for them to grow and develop from the egg or tadpole stages to full frogs. There is plenty of time for young children to observe and make sense of the changes, and enough going on in the tank to keep them engaged. In fact, this mini-habitat turns out to be a riveting life and death experience.

Sue uses dramatic play and puppetry, as well as visual and language arts experiences to help children find their own ways of expressing what they have observed. Notice also the role that nonfiction books play in the children's discovery process. The chapter ends with a field trip where children learn about the frogs' natural environment and return them there.

Plan to release the animals within a few days after they turn into full-fledged frogs. Before you start, be sure you have a place to release them. And check with a local expert about the kinds of frogs that exist locally.

HOW DO I BEGIN?

Before you bring the physical pieces together to create your tadpole habitat, it may be helpful to get an overview of what you may expect to see as you and your young observers examine the world of the ever-changing tadpoles and frogs. The narrative that recounts the experience in Sue's class starts with the tadpoles, which were approximately three to four weeks old. Although starting with frog *eggs* would have allowed the children an extended experience and offered important connections to the beginning of the life cycle, the older tadpoles attest to the excitement that these creatures bring to the class at whatever stage of development they are acquired. If you are lucky enough to find, or

buy, them in the egg stage, your tadpoles' development should look something like the following:
- The egg stage lasts one to 10 days; eggs hatch on approximately the tenth day.
- The back legs start to emerge at 5 to 6 weeks, and the front legs start to emerge after 8 to 10 weeks.
- The tail shortens and becomes a frog by 15 weeks.

Prior to hatching, the only maintenance the eggs need is fresh water. Use tap water that has been allowed to sit for about four hours or original pond water from the location you found the eggs. Living plants can help keep the water oxygenated.

When the eggs hatch, the tadpoles may be slow to take food. But within a few days, bloodworms (very thin, inch-long red worms) or creamed spinach will cause a fury of excitement in the tank as the ravenous young tadpoles compete for the food. In a pond water tank, living plants often accumulate algae, which is the natural food source for tadpoles.

As they become larger and stronger, the tadpoles will require more food and will afford the children extra opportunities to feed them. Water should be changed one to two times a week. Let the fresh water remain in an open container at least 6 hours before adding it to the tank. This brings the water to room temperature and allows some toxic (to tadpoles) chlorine additives to dissipate. Plants will allow children to see the algae-eating tadpoles feeding naturally.

When their legs begin to emerge, you and the children may notice the more developed frogs decrease in size and lose some strength. At this time, they may be attacked by larger and stronger tadpoles. You may choose to encourage your children to think and share their ideas about what kind of home an animal with legs may need. This can lead to setting up a second tank with both a water environment and rocks to climb upon. You may offer small crickets and flies as food to the maturing frogs.

A time will come when you and the children will release them to a natural environment. Returning them to the pond they came from is ideal. If you acquired them from a nature supply company, find out what kind of frog you have and check community sources (nature center, park or arboretum) for permission to release your kind of frog.

When you release them will depend on how well they are surviving in the mini-habitat. Many of the tadpoles that come from bio-supply companies are bred to live in conditions similar to our mini-habitats and thrive as adult frogs. Some tadpoles taken from local ponds will thrive in the tadpole stage but begin to become difficult eaters at the adult frog stage. They become listless and will eventually die. Releasing these frogs a few days after they mature or when they stop eating can be an important step in helping children see themselves as caretakers of nature. As children consider the options for a sick or listless frog they often will suggest a new home, thus setting the scene for a child initiated field trip to release the frogs. Whenever possible, wait for these cues for a meaningful next step. Providing a connection to the natural world by returning them to the pond they came from is ideal.

As you look over the narrative, you will see how Sue uses a child-centered discovery approach to help the children develop a more meaningful understanding of the changes they observe. Use your children's ideas about what to do next.

CREATING THE ENVIRONMENT

Stage I: Tadpoles

To create the tadpole mini-habitat, you will need:

Egg Strand or 4 to 5 Tadpoles
Available from a distributor. (See the resources at the end of the chapter for information.)

Aquarium
A standard glass aquarium placed at children's eye level works well. A plastic tank works, too, and is portable so you can take it outside for further observation.

Cheesecloth or Wire Mesh
Covering the aquarium will prevent the frogs from jumping out. Cover the aquarium early because frogs develop jumping ability very quickly.

Small Aquarium Plants
These give the tadpoles somewhere to hide and add oxygen to the environment. Don't add too many or it will be hard for children to find and observe the animals.

Bloodworms
This is the tadpoles' food. Available at pet stores or through a distributor.

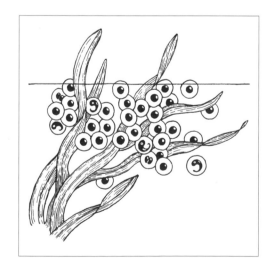

Reference Materials

Place books, posters, stories, etc., near the habitat. See suggestions at the end of this chapter.

Optional

Wall Space
For displaying children's work.

Stage II: Transition to Frogs

To create the frog mini-habitat, you will need all of the above, plus:

Aquarium

It is important to have a second tank available to separate the newly developing frogs from the tadpoles. You'll see why as you read what happened in Sue's class. Put less water in this one so the frogs can begin climbing out.

Hand-Sized Rock

Put these rocks in the aquarium so the frogs have something to jump up on.

Large Gravel (1/4" deep)

Use enough to cover the bottom of the second aquarium.

SUE'S STORY

The Story	*Steps and Teaching Tips*

Day 1

Before the children arrived, Sue provided a new mystery for her naturalists to discover. She set up a clear-sided plastic tank that held four two-week-old tadpoles.

Sue placed the tank on a table accompanied by two simple books that had many pictures of frogs and tadpoles. She did not tell the children about the new creatures. Instead, she sat near an earlier mini-habitat activity. Sue talked with a small group of children and used a ladybug puppet that added a great deal to the conversation. She did, however, keep one ear open so she could join the discussion when the children discovered the new aquarium and its inhabitants.

Once the children discovered the tank, they counted out loud to each other. Sue could hear, "There's one...two...three....four of them and they're in the water." "I think they are fish," stated Roxana with a bit of doubt in her voice.

Although the children were not sure what the animals were, there was much conversation about their shape, how they swam around the rocks, and "how big their heads were." The little "fish" had caught the children's attention. Sue wrote down their comments.

From their previous experiences, the children knew that the books Sue had left out would provide information about the animals in the tank. Soon, a few curious prereaders were flipping through the pages and pointing to recognizable figures like frogs and sharing those discoveries with a friend.

Put out a simple clear-sided tank with water and tadpoles or frog eggs. Set out a couple of frog books with clear photos next to the tank.

One way to stimulate children's interest is to let them discover something new in their classroom. Another way is to let the children help you prepare the aquarium for the tadpoles.

Write down or tape record children's comments. Post the notes near the tadpoles.

Encourage the children to use the reference books as resources.

Day 2

As the children came in the next day, many were drawn again to the developing tadpoles. Renewed interest in the books set many searching for pictures of the unidentified beings. After examining the many pictures in one book, Conrado asked Sue to read it, starting on the page with pictures that matched what he saw in the tank. Sue explained that animals in the picture were tadpoles.

This new information circulated through the class. Throughout the day as children stopped by to examine the tank, they heard about these tadpoles. When it was time to go home, E. J. used the grasshopper puppet to explain the discovery to his friend's big sister.

Continue to leave out reference books with clear pictures. Children will often ask you to read relevant information regarding the picture they have chosen. Keep it simple and let the story unfold at the children's pace. Let them make the connections.

Some children will get more practice speaking if they use puppets to speak for them. Experiment with puppets and see which of your children are drawn to them.

Now your tadpole experts can share their new knowledge with friends and visitors.

Day 3

Michael came straight into class and quickly checked out the nature table with the remains of the butterfly's chrysalis from last month's metamorphosis study. He reviewed them briefly and then darted over to the tadpole tank. As he examined it closely, he noticed a brownish red stringlike object floating in the water. Michael asked Sue to help him solve the mystery. As they watched together, more children came over to the tank. Sue encouraged suggestions on what it might be, validating all offerings as part of the group process of discovery.

While all this was going on, Maria shouted in amazement that the tadpole had eaten the string. This stimulated even more discussion. "So they like to eat these things." "They are food."

Questions of how they got the food and what it was soon surfaced. This provided Sue with an opportunity to share the book that came with the frogs, which told her about bloodworms.

Eric was sure the tadpoles were still hungry and should be fed. This was clearly the time to bring out the tadpoles' breakfast. Sue allowed each child to see, touch, and smell the frozen worms before she offered them to the tadpoles.

As the tadpoles grow larger, place bloodworms in the tank.

By placing worms in the tank, the children will discover what frogs eat. Add information about food sources as the children watch the hungry tadpoles.

Be sure you have some reference and story books out at this time. (Check the end of this chapter for suggestions.)

Allow the children to examine, touch, and smell the food.

The children watched with interest as the tadpoles attacked the lump of brown bloodworms. They talked and gestured excitedly as they described the tadpoles pulling and eating, swimming away, and using their fins to move.

Try to capture the children's comments as they express their excitement. Tape record or have other adults jot down words. Asking children about it later will help recall and expand language opportunities.

Day 5

As the days followed, the class discovered more about tadpoles. Jeanette discovered pages in one of the books that showed the sequenced growth of the tadpole as the tail shortens and legs grow out. This led Sue to read a story about how a baby tadpole had become a grown frog. Although it was hard to believe that these tadpoles might change to frogs, the book did say that they like bloodworms. When fed, they ate them so fast that A. J. exclaimed, "Boy, they sure like those bloodworms!"

Provide books with charts showing the sequenced growth of tadpole to frog.

Use colorful age appropriate literature to enhance the interest and compliment the reality of their experience.

Books are seen as important sources of information. Want to know? Find a book.

Day 7

During outside play before lunch and nap, Sue brought the tadpoles outside so the children could show (and describe) the flowers in the garden to them and tell them all about the big tree and the leaves.

Jonathan helped carry the paper and crayons outside so anyone who wanted could draw a picture of the frogs and their visit outside. Children from other classes soon joined them and drew pictures, also. Sue's class shared all they knew about tadpoles and frogs with the other children.

Bring the project outside. Many things we usually reserve for inside time can enrich the outside environment as well. And some children engage more easily during the less formal outside time. Help children make connections to other outdoor life forms. Bring the books outside, too: frogs jump on plants like these in the yard; frogs eat worms just like this one in the garden.

The recall that the children provided helped reinforce the concepts they knew and heightened their excitement for the project. Additional opportunity for language development and recall occurred as Sue wrote the children's words next to the tadpole pictures they had drawn.

Leave paper, markers, pencils, crayons, and other art materials out so the story of the tadpoles and frogs can be shared through pictures and drawings. As the children share their stories, record them with a tape recorder or write down their words and post them near their pictures. Some children will be ready to draw what they see. Drawing is an important tool many scientists use to sharpen their observational abilities and record what they see.

Your students are now the resident experts and can share their enthusiasm and knowledge with other children.

Day 10

The class became increasingly excited with the expectation of tadpoles changing to baby frogs and watched closely for evidence of change. E. J. made up several songs (as he did for most of the animals in the room) about how the "tadpole swims, swims and someday it will hop, hop, hop." Sue brought in a frog puppet. Mr. Frog led a discussion about the tadpole-to-frog chart Sue had put on the wall and about what the soon-to-appear frogs in the tank could eat.

Music is a natural medium for young children to express their love and excitement about nature. Encourage it. Or just sing any song with frog and tadpole information replacing the lyrics.

Sue engages children and extends the conversation by blending fantasy with accurate scientific information about frogs.

Day 15

The long-awaited proof that the tadpoles were indeed becoming frogs had finally arrived. Michael declared, "The tadpole has legs just like the one in the book."

Day 17

As the first tadpole began to change into a frog, it grew smaller and more vulnerable. The stronger and larger tadpoles attacked it. By the time the children saw him, he was dead and the other tadpoles were eating him. As the children made this discovery, they formed many suggestions as to what all this meant. They finally determined that the tadpoles thought the frog was food.

Many of the children were distressed about the dead frog. The class discussed what to do with it. A. J. suggested that he be buried outside. Another child said that he would be good for the garden. Without a great deal of ceremony the frog was placed in the ground near the hollyhocks. For some time after that, Sue, the children, and the frog puppet (and his friends Ladybug and Grasshopper) went out to talk to the garden. They told the story about how the frog had died and saw "how high he helped the hollyhocks grow."

Many changes—including death to more vulnerable tadpoles—happen as the tadpoles grow and develop. Try not to hide a death if it should occur. Allow the children to discover it and share possible causes and solutions.

Death is a normal part of any study of nature. When it happens, you have an opportunity to help children with this "tender topic." Provide opportunities to talk. Then follow their lead on deciding what and how much to do.

Day 18

After the death of the first frog, the children expressed their concern for what would happen to those that followed. "When they get legs they get ate." This led to an opportunity for the children to plan what they could do to help the new frogs.

Christian suggested that the baby frogs needed a new home. Responding to this innovative idea, Sue provided a duplicate habitat environment. She gave Christian the job of choosing which tadpoles should be moved to the new home. He and other interested children assisted in the transfer by preparing the environment.

Encourage the children to share their feelings and ideas about the unfortunate death of animals in their care. This can lead you and them to consider ways to prevent such occurrences.

When the tadpoles are almost frogs, prepare the second aquarium.

Day 28

In the following 10 days, the back and then the front legs of the frog that had been moved developed. He flourished in his solitary environment. The day the tadpole became a full-fledged frog and jumped onto the big rock, anyone in the room could see the leap of faith Christian took in his own ability to solve problems and make a difference. His idea had worked!

New and good ideas emerge from children when they have authentic opportunities to solve meaningful problems. You can be most effective by providing the things they need to carry out their plans.

Day 33

The fully developed frogs were becoming weak with their reluctance to eat the variety of food that both Sue and the children offered to them.

After one died, there was a group discussion of what to do to help them. Gabrielle suggested that the frogs should be let go.

Sue took the children on a walking field trip to a nearby pond. As they embarked on their trip, they passed by the elementary group. When the boys playing ball asked Sue where their group was going, she asked the children to explain about the frogs and the pond. The children had two more opportunities to be experts when they passed the city worker, and when they were introduced to the director of the nature center who would take care of their frogs. The director welcomed the children when they explained what kind of frogs they had.

Sue took pictures of the frogs and their new home so everyone could remember them. She placed the frogs near the pond and then everyone said goodbye.

When you release your young frogs, return them to the environment from which you got the tadpoles or make sure that the caretakers of the new habitat are aware of what kind of frog you have. If you have purchased your frog eggs or tadpoles from a nature supply company, call the supplier for information on where to release your frogs.

Day 34

After nap, one of the girls spontaneously began what she called a "Frog Train." Soon all the children—and Sue—were on the train on their way to the pond. As part of the trip, they retold the story of their experience with the tadpoles and frogs.

Photographs are wonderful ways of helping children recall their experiences. They also help build class cohesion by reminding children of their shared experiences.

Field Trips

Field trip opportunities can include visiting a neighborhood park with a pond, a neighborhood resident with a backyard pond, a nature center with aquatic displays inside or a pond outside, an arboretum, botanical gardens, a zoo, or even an office building with a pond or aquatic environment as part of its landscape. All of these places are terrific for supporting the study in the mini-habitat as it is going on, or as preparation to bringing the habitat into the classroom.

Reference books

Amazing Frogs and Toads — Eyewitness Juniors by Barry Clarke, Alfred A. Knopf, 1990.

Keeping Minibeasts — Frogs by Chris Henwood, Franklin Watts, 1988.

Tadpole and Frog by Christine Back and Barrie Watts, Stopwatch, Silver Burdett Press, 1984.

The World of Frogs and Toads by Jane Dallinger and Sylvia Johnson, Lerner Publications, 1982.

See How They Grow, Frog by Kim Taylor, Lodestar Books, 1991.

Frog by Moira Butterfield, Simon and Schuster, 1992.

Peterson First Guide to Reptiles and Amphibians by Roger Conant, Houghton Mifflin Company, 1992.

Resources

Acorn Naturalists
17300 East 17th Street #J-236
Tustin, CA 92680
(800-422-8886)
(800-452-2802) FAX

Insect Lore Products
P.O. Box 1535
Shafter, CA 93263
(800 Live Bug)
(805 746-6047)

Contact this nature supply company for information on obtaining animal species, support materials, and books.

Silver Burdett Press (Stopwatch Series)
P.O. Box 2649
Columbus, OH 43216
(800-848-9500)

Stories

Frog and Toad Are Friends by Arnold Lobel, Harper Collins, 1978.

Frog Frog Frog by Robert Welber, Pantheon, 1971.

Jump, Frog, Jump! by Robert Kalan, Greenwillow, 1981.

What Made Tiddalik Laugh by Joanna Troughton, Bedrick/Blackie, 1986.

The Caterpillar and the Polliwog by Jack Kent, Simon and Schuster Books for Young Readers, 1982.

Frog and Birdsong by Max Velthuijs, Farrar, Straus and Giroux, 1991.

Poems

"Haiku" by Yayu from *Tomie DePaola's Book of Poems*, Putnam, 1988.

"The Soggy Frog" from *The Sheriff of Rottenshot: Poems*, by Jack Prelutsky, Greenwillow, 1982.

Earthworms

INTRODUCTION

Earthworms are a wonderful way to let children see a full life cycle and to understand more about the food chain and the complex world that exists underground. Children can become quite involved with earthworms, starting with their first touch of the cool soil and the sensation of a worm crawling on their hands. Soon, they'll discover tiny underground hatcheries filled with baby worms and observe the nocturnal creatures burrowing away from the light.

Not everyone likes the feeling of worms right away. Notice how Sue creates many different ways of being involved in the project and learning about the worms. She also leaves time for children—and adults—to explore at their own pace. Our experience has been that teachers can do this unit even if they don't like to touch worms themselves. There's always someone in the class who will enjoy working with the worms and the soil.

Of the most satisfying benefits Sue's class received from this experience was the opportunity for the children to participate in the recycling activity of composting. Since the worms' food source is leftover table scraps, the children delighted in feeding the worms and watching their crackers and cheese turn into new soil for the plants in the garden.

Notice how Sue deftly ties together indoor and outdoor activities, written material, a field trip, and children's previous experiences to create a unified whole. It's not fancy teaching, but it matches beautifully the way young children learn.

HOW DO I BEGIN?

Earthworms are one of the most easily maintained habitats. If the worms are not readily available in your yard or garden, use red worms found at the local bait and tackle shop.

Creating a worm habitat will be a joy for your children as they get a first-hand tactile experience of the world of worms while putting together the mixture of peat moss, soil, and water into a well-ventilated container. Keeping the worms cool and moist is important.

Food for the worms can best come from the suggestions of the children. Encourage them to try everything from leaves to birthday cake.

Within the first 2 to 4 weeks, you can anticipate many discoveries, including worm eggs, baby worms, and the hard, tubelike castings that provide nutrients back to the soil.

As you follow the narrative, notice the questions Sue's children expressed and answers they found through their own observation and experimentation and at their own pace. You'll see how the children helped each other and their parents to overcome fear or concern about the worms.

The growth and development of worms consists of the egg stage in egg cocoons, which lasts for 2 weeks. Very small, threadlike worms emerge and steadily increase in size over approximately 2 months. The grown worms mate. Each worm is both male and female; both mated worms lay new cocoons.

CREATING THE ENVIRONMENT

To create the earthworm mini-habitat, you will need:

Earthworms

For a class of 25, you will need about 50 worms, though the number is not that important. You and your class can dig them yourselves. Worms are also available at bait and tackle shops. Red worms work well.

Containers

For the first day: One or two shallow cardboard boxes or cardboard box tops.

Permanent Home (two options)

1) Plastic storage container about 4" high and 2-1/2' x 1-1/2' works best, but you can use any size that will fit on your table. The advantage of this container is that children can see around all sides. Drill or punch some holes in the bottom for air and drainage.

2) Wooden box of a similar size. (You could build the box as a group project.) This will also work, though the children won't be able to see as well.

Lid for container. Whether you use a plastic container or a wooden box, you will need a lid. Keep the lid on when children are not viewing the worms. This helps keep the environment dark and moist. When the container is outside, the lid also protects the worms from predators. However, if you are using a solid lid, cut out a large hole in the center and cover it with screening or cheesecloth. Worms are sensitive to heat and need ventilation.

Soil Mixture

Although there are many worm bed mixtures, one that works well includes soil mixture, shredded newspaper, and water. Using the universal measuring tool of a small (1 lb.) coffee can the ingredients should be combined in a ratio of:

> 4 cans of compacted compost or topsoil to
> 1 can of water
> 2-3 sheets of shredded paper (shredded by the children)

For the soil, organic compost or organic topsoil from a gardening store works well. But any soil, including dirt from your yard, will do. You will need a bucket or wheelbarrow to mix this all together. Let the children help you. Many will enjoy the gooey feeling of the soil mixing together.

Food

Table leftovers are best, as you will see in more detail in the narrative. Also, check the reference book *Worms Eat My Garbage* (listed at the end of this unit) for other food suggestions.

Reference Materials

Books (see suggestions at the end of this chapter), posters, and charts. Place these near the habitat with writing and drawing materials.

When leaving the worm bed over the weekend, or even overnight, be sure to leave it in a cool place—low to the ground and dark. When doors and windows are closed, heat can rise, and worms can get overheated and die.

THE WORMS IN SUE'S CLASS

The Story	*Steps and Teaching Tips*

When Sue and her class worked in the school garden, they had noticed the earthworms as they cultivated the dirt. Sue decided it was time for the children to learn more about them.

She began by searching for earthworms in a large unplanted spot of the garden, in her backyard, and in a similar spot in the play yard at school. Although she found some worms, Sue realized that she would have to supplement them with the red worms from a bait and tackle shop. 50 worms seemed to be about the right number.

> **Look for earthworms in your yard or neighborhood. You will need a large number of them to get the project going, so you will probably have to buy some as well.**

Sue housed the worms in 2 shallow cardboard boxes. (Actually, they were lids from produce boxes.) Filled with moistened peat moss and worms, these temporary habitat environments were ready for the children to explore.

> **Start the worms in shallow boxes filled with moistened peat moss. The shallow containers make the worms easier to find.**

Day 1

It was now almost a week since the children had taken the walking field trip to release the frogs. (See the chapter "Tadpoles to Frogs.") The now empty frog tank and books were still on display. A. J. and Michael began the morning reliving part of the experience using the puppets.

> **Leave items from past projects available to the children for a while. They help them recall their experiences.**

Sue brought the two boxes of worms to a table. She took out scissors, glue, and magazine pictures of ants and worms and began decorating the boxes. Michael and A. J. came over to see what was happening.

"There's dirt in this box!" exclaimed Michael as he ran his fingers over the top of the cool, lightly moistened soil. "That's right, Michael, this box of dirt is called soil," Sue confirmed. "What do you think you might find in the dirt or soil?"

Soon others joined the conversation and added suggestions about what they might find.

Almost unconsciously, some children began running their fingers through the soil. Others participated in the conversation, but were still a little reserved about putting their hands in.

Sue knew it wouldn't take long for someone to discover a worm. Roberto had the honor of holding up the first earthworm and exclaiming, "Lombreis," which means worm in Spanish.

Soon, children were crowded around the two cartons. Many searched the dirt for other worms. Others were happy to watch.

Sue established some simple ground rules to control the crowd, protect the worms, and maintain hygiene standards. The lid (at this stage a simple, airy cloth) needed to stay over the box. Children could lift the lid and look in the box at any time. But they could only hold the worms when an adult was present. "We don't want to hold them too much," Sue explained.

"Elliot, why do you think we don't want to touch the worms all the time?" Sue asked. "Because they might get mad and bite me," he responded.

Sue took this opportunity to dispel Elliot's concern, which she assumed was the unspoken concern of others as well. "Let's look at one of the earthworms more closely," she said, "Now, what do we need to bite our food?" After the group chanted, "teeth," they inspected the worm. Although opinions varied on which end was the head, no one could find teeth.

After that valuable digression, Sue decided that the worms had been touched enough and needed to rest. "Good night worms. Have a good rest," said children as they laid the cloth over the box.

The boxes stimulate conversation and interest. Sue draws out children's existing knowledge and experience around dirt. This helps them connect with the materials and encourages prediction and, simply, more conversation.

Children will differ in their interest in touching the soil—and the worms. This is to be expected. As excitement builds, more and more children will participate physically, though some may never want to. Don't push. There are many other ways to know and experience the world.

Sue lets the children discover the worms. Discovery is an exciting way for children to learn, but you could introduce the mini-habitats in other ways as well.

Establish simple rules:

1) Keep the cover on except while viewing or holding the worms.

2) Moisten hands and limit holding times. (Worms breathe through their skin and must remain moist and cool to survive.)

3) Wash hands after handling.

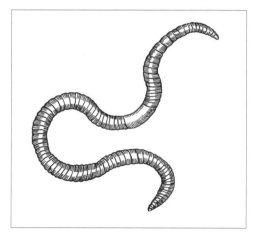

Children may have unexpected fears of unfamiliar animals. It is likely that if one child expresses a fear, others harbor the same—or similar—concerns as well. Information and guided exploration are the best ways to help children overcome their fears. In this example, Sue validates their concerns while giving them the experiences and knowledge that help children overcome them.

Day 2

Sue suspected that the first thing on the minds of many of the children this morning would be earthworms. So she let the children take them out of the box and inspect them. She put a piece of plastic out on the table near the worm box. She supervised as children carefully removed the worms and put them on the plastic. Taking the worms out of the soil for a little while allowed the children to observe their shapes and movements more easily.

The worms needed a larger, more permanent container. Sue encouraged the children to help her prepare the new home.

Outside, the soil was in a barrel, ready for shoveling, the premeasured water was in the bucket, and newspaper was ready for shredding.

Sue organized and supervised the project but her crew did the work. They combined the worm bed materials in a separate container for thorough mixing.

Before the children shoveled the soil into a large clear plastic container, Sue let everyone look closely to notice the holes in the

Although worms will dry out if they are out of soil too long, you can put them out for short periods. Place plastic over a table and moisten the surface before you put the worms down. Allow the children to take the worms from the container for close observation. Have writing and drawing materials nearby and help children record their experiences.

Get the children involved in making the permanent environment.

Have soil, newspaper, and water ready. You'll need an extra container to mix the ingredients together.

bottom. Then they discussed the need for all animals—even animals who live underground—to have air to breathe.

Many wondered if the worms would crawl away. Sue admitted it might happen and suggested they keep an eye on what the earthworms do.

Once the mixture was ready, it was time to see how the worms liked their new home. The children carefully took handfuls of wigglers and placed them on the surface of the soil. They watched with great interest. The worms were "making a hole and going underneath." "They like to be way down in the ground." After this, the children spent some time gently searching for worms near the bottom and bringing them on top for better inspection. The clear plastic sides of the worms' new home provided a glimpse of their behavior, though their aversion to light kept them away from the edges.

Place worms in a permanent container. Allow the children to observe the worms as they acclimate.

Day 4

She knew that the fresh peat moss had provided enough nutrients for the worms, but they would soon need other food. Late that morning during outside time, she lifted up one of the worms from the new box and said, "You know, Mr. Worm, I can't wait to eat my lunch today. I am very hungry." Rosalind chimed in that Mr. Worm needs his snack. "Well, Mr. Earthworm," said Sue, "what do you eat?" An examination of the peat moss gave some cues. After discussing the suggested food sources for worms, Anthony and Rebecca went with E. J. to pick leaves and grass.

When they returned, Sue suggested they put only two items on top of the soil to see which one the worms would eat.

At lunch the discussion about what worms eat brought in suggestions from children who had not been involved outside. When crackers and cheese were left over, Sarah wanted to feed them to the worms. Sue decided it would be interesting to give the worms some choices. They decided that after nap, the worms would be fed crackers and cheese as well.

Worms pull their food down underground and then process it, so the children couldn't actually observe the worms eating. They would have to wait to see what the worms chose.

The worms will need food. Encourage discussion of possible choices.

Notice how some of the best discussion—and involvement—comes over lunch rather than at "science time." Children don't divide up the world into tidy subject areas and time slots. Make use of the opportunities and connections that arise.

The discussion led to a kind of scientific experiment. Note how Sue's earlier suggestion that they limit what they offer the worms and watch what happens sets the stage for Sarah's planned investigation.

Day 5

The children checked the worms' box. It was too early to tell what the worms had eaten. They decided to leave the food alone and check later.

A number of children gathered around the table and carefully took out worms to observe. Sue put inexpensive magnifiers at the table, which the children used eagerly.

Patience is one of the virtues developed in observing nature. Worms do not rush through their meals.

Put magnifiers out at the tables. In using them, children not only learn more about the worms, they learn about using tools to assist in observation. This is an important part of learning to "do" science.

Day 6

The first question on Conrado's mind and out of his mouth was, "Did the worms eat yet?" "Well," Sue suggested, "let's look and see."

When they took the lid off the worm box, the crackers were gone, and the cheese was dirty and only a third as big as it started. They had found something the worms eat.

Check the box and see what the worms have eaten. You can create a chart or graph of the information.

The children helped Sue bring the worm bed out during play time. They shared the news with the classes playing outside. This generated a great deal of discussion and worm examination, with the children from Sue's class taking the expert roles. The children planned to continue their experiment by saving leftovers from their lunches. They added these to the box.

Create opportunities for children to share their new knowledge. It's good for children to be experts about things— they learn themselves by telling others. We know from research that, in the relationship between tutors and tutees, the tutors are the ones who learn the most.

Continue to add food for the worms. Let the children take charge. This keeps interest high and allows for more experimenting.

Day 8

More food was missing, which delighted the children. When discussing this second successful episode, Sue brought up the word "composting" and described how soil was made from food leftovers and leaves and grass. She asked if anyone thought the worms help composting. A few agreed that worms eat the garbage and make it go away; they make it into soil.

After the children have seen the worms make the food into soil, you can give the process a name: composting.

Day 10

Sue found a helpful chart of the foods worms generally eat in the book, *Worms Eat My Garbage*. She enlarged the list because the pictures alongside the food items would help interpret the words listed on the sheet.

What came about was an unexpected and wonderful skill development activity.

At morning snack, Sue brought the poster of "What Worms Like to Eat" to the children's attention. She pointed out each food item. The children were pleased about the ones they had already tried. After that, the day was filled with one child after another sharing what the list said and using the picture cues. "I know worms eat spaghetti, I know worms eat birthday cake and they eat corn." They pointed to the word identified with the object. It was certainly an enthusiastic learning exercise that was totally unplanned.

In the days that followed, when any of these items came into the classroom, one of the children would run to the chart and tell the class that worms eat it.

In learning to read, it's important to know the alphabet. But, it's just as important to learn how information—in print and on paper—relates to concrete experiences. In experiences like this one, children learn just those kinds of relationships. Knowing that reading is an exciting, meaningful act that informs other experiences is a key factor in "reading readiness."

Day 12

On this afternoon, Mariana, dressed in white lace and chiffon, was thoroughly engaged with a worm she held dangling from her thumb and forefinger, talking to it in a mix of Spanish and English.

Mariana's mother walked into the school and saw her daughter with the worms. Mariana caught a glimpse of her mother and called to her to come over. Her mother, who did not like worms, hesitated, and asked Mariana to come to her so they could go home.

Sue stepped in and explained that Mariana was excited about her new interest and wanted to show the worms to her mother. Reluctantly, Mariana's mother came closer and Mariana said, "See, Mama, it doesn't bite me." With a hesitant laugh, Mariana's mother came closer for a look.

After that, Mariana shared her nature discoveries with her mother. And her mother, though she never became a lover of small wiggly creatures, became less hesitant to observe and participate.

Bringing parents closer to your program and what their children experience is a big challenge for many teachers. A child's high level of interest in nature activities draws the caring parent in for a closer look. Note the skill Sue displays in noticing the parent's discomfort and helping Mariana make her mother more comfortable.

Day 18

Mathew noticed light tan, hard tubelike things in the mini-habitat and asked Sue what they were. Sue didn't know, so she sat down with everyone and looked in the book about earthworms. They found a picture and learned that the tubes were the waste of the worm. The tubes were castings and they made the soil healthy for the plants.

You don't have to be an expert to do these units. If you know an answer to a child's question, answer it. If not, it's good for them to see you using books and charts as references. They learn that no one has all the answers, but everyone can search them out, and books are a good place to look.

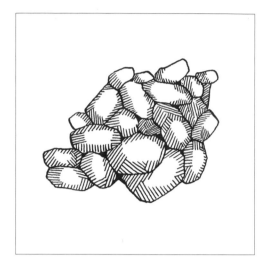

Day 21

As the children examined the soil regularly, seeing pieces of crackers, bread, and carrots turn to soil "for the plants," they also noticed little round balls. No one was sure what they were. Conrado looked at *Earthworms*, one of the reference books that was near the worm box. He saw a drawing that looked like the little balls. Conrado asked Sue to come and see. She did, and read that the round balls were worm egg cases. Soon baby worms would hatch.

Again, the reference books play a critical role in discovery. Note how this time the children use the book to help them anticipate what will happen. Along with learning to love nature, they are having subtle yet important prereading experiences.

Day 25

Today Sue and the children carried the worm box outside. Someone had left a worm out of the box, and it fell off the table. As the class watched, a bird swooped down, scooped up the worm, and flew off.

The class talked about worms being food for animals. What other animals eat worms? Jesse went fishing with his grandfather and used worms. Caroline remembered how the tadpoles devoured bloodworms.

Unexpected events present the opportunity to help children make meaningful connections between past experiences and the current habitat study.

Here, Sue takes the opportunity to put the worms into their natural context and connect the project with children's experiences with a lesson on the worm's place in the food chain.

Day 30

Today Anthony discovered the baby worms. They were tiny and threadlike. Everyone was fascinated by this big clump of wiggles. A. J. said he thought they looked like the bloodworms for the tadpoles. He suggested that the class take some to the frogs at the pond.

With this new birth came a renewed interest in singing about the birds, worms, and frogs. Sue brought out her guitar, and she and the children made up a song. E. J. even added a worm dance.

Watch for the baby worms. Notice how much conversation their birth stimulates. In this case, the children begin to connect the baby worms with previous experiences. As always, have materials on hand to help them record their ideas.

Music is a mode of expression that comes naturally to most children. You don't need a song expressly about worms. You can make one up. Use tunes the children are already familiar with, and change the words. Once you get started, the children will do most of the work.

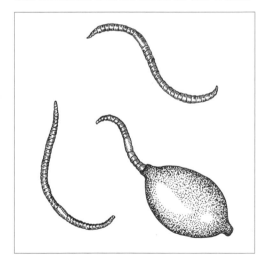

Day 35

Once the babies were born, the cycle was complete. When the time came for planting in the garden, and soil needed to be enriched, Sue asked, "What do we need to make our garden healthy?" This led to a discussion of what to do to make the soil healthy. Melissa suggested that the worms could make new soil. So the worms were dumped in

Try to bring the idea full circle. If worms make soil, then let the children suggest that the worms help make the soil for a garden. If not a school garden,

the garden (all except 5 that were saved to feed the frogs). The children watched and said good bye, warned the worms to be careful of the birds, and let them vanish underground.

When they had all disappeared, Michael brought over a small pile of leaves to help them make soil.

Day 37

Sue arranged a trip back to the pond where the class had released the frogs. The children took a small box with 5 worms to give to the frogs so they, too, could grow. That's what worms do—they help many things grow: plants, birds, and frogs.

After the walk, and after nap time, the trip was the focus of play. Everyone sat down on the rug, and as they put their shoes on, they formed a train. Everyone became the worm train going to see the frogs. Sue was right in one of the middle cars. She and the children sang about the frogs and worms and how they get the soil to the garden.

then a neighbor's garden or planter boxes. When the flowers grow, the children will remember the worms.

For young children, dramatic play is an important method of organizing and understanding the world. Encourage it. Some teachers are comfortable participating in the play and can do it without directing it or taking it over. Other teachers are more comfortable and effective watching children play and providing what's necessary to keep it going.

Field Trips

Field trip opportunities to search for earthworms (and other underground creatures) start as close as your yard and anywhere you have the owner's permission to till the soil. Since you don't want to disrupt a grassy landscape, dig around the perimeter and under bushes and trees. A neighbor might even donate a patch of ground. More and more communities use earthworms in their composting efforts, and they may be able to accommodate your group for a field trip. If you started your worm bed from a bait and tackle shop, ask them where they get their worms and check to see if it is an appropriate preschool field trip site. Vacant lots or nearby natural areas can provide generous settings for underground exploration. Moist soil provides the best results. The rich soil near ponds and lakes can provide interesting investigation. When it rains, the worms often make their way to sidewalks and asphalt, providing your children easy viewing, collection, and maybe some ideas on where they came from before the rain.

Reference Books

Earthworms—Junior Science by Terry Jennings, Gloucester Press, 1990.

Worms Eat My Garbage by Mary Appelhof, Flower Press, 1982.

Keeping Minibeasts—Earthworms by Chris Henwood, Franklin Watts, 1988.

Wonderful Worms by Linda Glaser, The Millbrook Press, 1992.

Earthworm by Andrienne Soutter-Perrot, Creative Editions, 1993.

My First Nature Book by Angela Wilkes, Alfred A. Knopf, Inc., 1990.

Resources

Insect Lore Products
P.O. Box 1535
Shafter, CA 93263
(800 Live Bug)
(805 746-6047)
Contact this nature supply company for information on obtaining animal species, support materials, and books.

Acorn Naturalists
17300 East 17th Street #J-236
Tustin, CA 92680
(800-422-8886)
(800-452-2802) FAX

BioQuip
17803 LaSalle Avenue
Gardena, CA 90248
(310 324-0620)
(310 324-7931) FAX

Silver Burdett Press (Stopwatch Series)
P.O. Box 2649
Columbus, OH 43216
(800-848-9500)

The Worm Concern, for live worms and helpful information on composting.
(805 496-2872)

Poems

"Under the Ground" by Rhoda W. Bacmeister, from *Read-Aloud Rhymes for the Very Young*, selected by Jack Prelutsky, Knopf, 1986.

"Worm" by Mary Ann Hoberman, from *The Poetry Troupe: An Anthology of Poems To Read Aloud*, compiled by Isabel Wilner, Scribner, 1977.

Praying Mantises

INTRODUCTION

The praying mantis project focuses on an insect habitat that provides a window to nature. You will see children's involvement and interest grow with the mantises, which begin as inert egg cases. From the cases emerge hundreds of tiny, energetic insects. As these carnivorous creatures grow and develop, they will depend on your children for help in acquiring their food.

Learning about the connection and interdependency of plants and animals comes naturally as children see how small aphids eat plants, and how, in turn, the larger praying mantises need the aphids to live. The concepts of life cycle and food chain arise through observation and active participation.

In the narrative that follows, Beth involves the children in preparing the habitat. This gives them an activity to do while they wait for new developments. It also helps them feel more involved and responsible.

HOW DO I BEGIN?

Before you order your praying mantis egg case from a distributor, scout your local aphid population. Roses and citrus trees are often plagued with these tiny mantis edibles.

Setting the stem of the aphid-infested branch in water will keep the aphids thriving and extend the food source for the mantises. Don't leave too much water exposed as baby mantises drown easily.

Once the praying mantis egg case arrives, let your children help create an environment. Use a windowed box (a cardboard box with clear plastic portholes) to hold a small branch from one of the aphid-infested

plants. Include a shallow container for water.

Gently attach the egg case with string to the branch; wait and watch what happens. Children will be watching the egg case for new arrivals. Make sure reference materials are available.

When the small, new-born mantises emerge from the sack, they will hang from glossy, somewhat gooey amber strings. As they dry, they will hop on the leaves of the branch and begin looking for aphid food. It is easy to see that their little brown forms are almost identical to their grown parents. They differ mostly in color and size.

As they grow and molt, your mantises will show your

children how they shed their outside skeleton and emerge each time closer to their adult color and size. The grown praying mantis' green color hides him well on the leaf where he waits, and helps him successfully hunt his aphid (and other insect) prey.

Praying mantises are fun to watch. You will soon hear much language and dramatic play being shared about body parts and movement as your children become experts on how insects move and hunt.

Notice as you read the following narrative how Beth allows her children to lead her on a search for mantis food, which reinforces concepts on the food chain and leads to new insect discoveries. The most meaningful discoveries often occur when you look for one thing and happen upon some other thing.

The growth and development timeline of your praying mantises will be something like this:

- Hatching is normally one to three weeks after delivery. Check with the distributor as hatching will depend on the species and the conditions in which the egg case was stored.

- Emergence from the egg case may last one to two days. Each mantis will hang on a silklike thread in a crystal sack for about an hour while their outside skeletons harden.

- The first molt occurs after one month. Six to nine molts will follow. The frequency and number of molts will depend on how much food the mantises eat and how fast they grow.

- Wings will start to emerge after two months, but flight will not be possible at this stage.

- The last molt occurs after three to four months. A full-grown mantis will have its full-size wings and will be able to fly. Mating and egg laying will also be possible.

CREATING THE ENVIRONMENT

Stage I: Gentle Exploration

To create the praying mantis mini-habitat, you will need:

Praying Mantis Egg Case

Order yours from a biosupply house (see the end of the chapter for sources). The egg case is a ball about 2" x 1". The outside is light brown and made of crinkly material. **All you need at first is a shallow box, such as a shoe box.** This provides a closer look for the children and teacher-supervised opportunities for exploring the egg case.

Once the children have looked at—and gently touched—the egg case, let them know that it is time for the egg case to rest and that it will need a new home.

Stage II: Hatching and Growing

Habitat (three options)

1) Window viewing box (24" cube) available through nature supply companies (see the list at the end of the chapter for sources).

2) Standard aquarium (glass or plastic) covered with screening for ventilation.

3) Home-made viewing box made from a cardboard box (2' x 2' x 2'). Cut large circles in the sides and replace them with a sturdy transparent plastic or screening material. At least one window needs to have screening for ventilation. Enlist the help of the children to create the box or at least decorate the cardboard before windows are cut out and screened.

Put in the habitat:

- Small branch or stem with leaves. Try to find branches with aphids on the leaves. If you find the aphids, place the branch in water. The aphids will die if the leaves dry out. And if the aphids die, the young mantises will eat each other. You will need to replace the branch several times during the mantises' lives.

- A couple of hand-sized rocks.

Water

Small shallow water bowl (a jar lid is fine); baby mantises easily drown, so don't add too much water.

Food

For the first month, the young mantises need aphids. (In Southern California, these are, unfortunately, all too easy to find most of the year, though they're more prevalent when the weather is warmer.) Before beginning, be sure you can find a supply of aphids either in your neighborhood or through a distributor.

Older mantises will also eat crickets and flies (crickets are available at pet stores).

Spray Bottle

Misting the egg case occasionally helps keep the mantises alive. Keep the misting light, though.

Reference Materials

Books (see suggestions at the end of this chapter), posters, charts, magnifiers. Place these near the habitat with writing and drawing materials.

PRAYING MANTISES IN BETH'S CLASS

The Story

Beth knew she would be unlikely to find a praying mantis egg case in a natural setting. Even if she could, she would not want to remove it. She ordered her egg cases from a nature supply company.

The mantis eggs arrived about four weeks before they were to hatch. Not wanting the time before hatching to seem endless, Beth waited until a week before their due date before introducing the egg case to her class.

Steps and Teaching Tips

For the names and addresses of nature education supply companies, see the resource section at the end of this chapter.

Read the information enclosed with the specimens to determine dates for introduction.

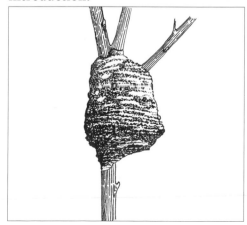

Day 1

Before bringing in the egg case, Beth brought out many pictures of insects, including praying mantises. She asked the children to paste the pictures onto a small shoe box.

The activity stimulated conversation about insects. Children shared their knowledge of and experiences with insects and did impressions. None of the children knew the name of the insects with "the big buggy eyes." Beth told them they were praying mantises.

At story time, Christina chose a grasshopper story from the book corner and asked Beth to read it.

The shoe box was left out for the rest of day for examination, and Beth read from Christina's book on grasshoppers.

Prepare children with materials and activities that involve discussion of insects.

Listen to children's casual conversations during work time. You'll learn what they understand. You can also help them build connections to the projects you present.

Beth tells the children the insect's name. Although many teachers believe in discovery learning, young children can't discover the names of things.

Children learn through stories as well as through experience. Children's literature is an important adjunct to nature study.

Day 2

The next morning, Beth sat at a table where children were using natural materials to make collage art. She brought out the box the children had decorated the day before. Inside was the tan, hardened foam mass that held about 100 baby praying mantises.

Beth took the egg case out and put it on the lid of the box, telling everyone how fragile it was. She would be the only one to take it out, but asked, "Would anyone like to give a gentle one finger touch?" Under close supervision, some of the children felt the strange texture. (Beth would have preferred a more relaxed, less supervised format, but everyone seemed to understand that the egg case was fragile and needed to be kept safe.)

Magnifiers were available nearby, and the children naturally brought these over to assist in observation.

Decorating a box, yesterday's art activity becomes today's home for the egg case.

Place yourself in an inviting situation. Let the children come to you motivated by their own interest.

We want children to be eager to explore the natural world. However, it's also important for them to know when to be cautious—both for their own sakes and for nature's. It's important to give them clear directions about when and how to explore.

Make magnifiers, collection boxes, and nature guides a regular part of your class. Using these tools of science and literacy will become everyday events for children. This is as critical in preparing them for reading as teaching them the alphabet!

Day 4

The children checked the egg case for any changes. They tried to connect what they had learned from the reference materials about baby praying mantises coming out of this piece of foam, but it was hard.

Children need lots of opportunities to repeat their observations and to connect the things they learn from books

Beth knew from the materials that accompanied the egg case that the babies would be hatching soon. She suggested that "We could help the praying mantises by making a nature home in the classroom." She brought out a large box and markers, so anyone who wanted could draw on the box. Later, she cut big holes on three sides. Beth let the children help attach the sturdy clear plastic sheets to the inside of the box with glue and tape.

with those they know from personal experiences. Don't be afraid to repeat experiences.

If you construct your own habitat, let children assist you. But be sure in the end the box is sturdy and enclosed enough to hold and protect the insects.

Day 5

The new home needed only a living tree branch with an ample supply of aphids.

Beth had scouted out the area earlier to see what the aphid population was like. Luckily, she had found an orange tree that was infested with aphids. She had also checked with neighbors, friends, and relatives. She had a few back-up supplies from friends who were glad to give up their aphids.

That morning, Beth discussed with the children how they were going out to look for aphids, the tiny insects praying mantises eat. She told them that aphids live in trees and "sometimes the tree can tell us if aphids live in them. When aphids live in trees, the trees roll up their leaves. The aphids can kill the trees."

The search was successful. Manuel discovered a branch on the orange tree that had curly leaves. Beth carefully cut a branch and put it in a plastic bag.

Back in class, Beth took a few leaves off the branch and put them in a shallow box. With magnifiers in hand, her young investigators got their first glimpse of aphids.

After snack, Beth set the branch (now cut to fit) diagonally in the box; the closely knit small branches cradled the egg case. The stage was now set for the emergence of the baby mantises.

Your mini-habitat needs a branch and some aphids to be complete.

Check out trees with aphids beforehand, then go on a hunt with your children. If it's cold, however, you may have trouble finding aphids.

Have a back-up food source. This would be a good time to enlist the help of parents. Send a note home asking them to send in aphid-infested branches. Be sure they're in plastic bags. You don't want to introduce aphids to a place that doesn't already have them.

An aphid search gives children the chance to look closely at parts of the world they see every day. Learning which plants do and do not have aphids helps build a deeper understanding of their environment.

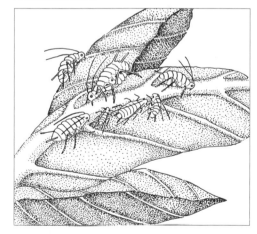

Give children a chance to investigate the aphids separately and close-up. Have magnifiers available.

Place the egg case, the branch with aphids, and a small container of water or damp sponge in the mini-habitat. Cover the habitat. You don't want to introduce aphids to any of the other plants you may have in your classroom.

Day 8

Despite regular checking, nothing had happened for three days. This morning, however, when Jonathan went over to look, he found what the class had been waiting for. He stood watching a wet mantis baby emerge from the egg case. Beth noticed Jonathan's absorption and went over to see what was happening. She was pleased to see that the first small insects were emerging.

As the baby praying mantises dried, the children watched in amazement while the newborn insects made their way about their new environment.

As the insects emerge, help children record their reactions. It's a good time to take dictation from children or put drawing materials out nearby. Post their work near the observation area. After all the mantises have hatched, you can make their work into a book about the births. Put the book in your classroom library. You'll be amazed how much the children use it and recall their shared experiences.

Day 9

The children spent much time observing these distinctive insects. Their large eyes, cocked heads, and front-leg "praying" motion make them fun to watch. Mantises continued to hatch throughout the day.

The mantises have presented some important lessons on insects to the children. As with most insects, hundreds of eggs are enclosed in a single casing. But the attrition rate is high. The children witnessed for themselves the ones that drowned, that never unfurled from the casing, and that died because they were not strong enough. Beth explained that it is normal in the insect world to lay many eggs so that some will be assured of survival. This helped ease any concern and sadness.

Though many babies died, the children were happy to see that the healthy mantises gobbled up the aphid food that the children had found for them.

These creatures are engaging. This provides more natural opportunities for children to record their impressions. Invite a parent to take dictation. Or use the tape recorder to tape children's observations.

Many insects will die at or near birth. This is a good time to discuss how insect species survive by having high birth-rates.

Day 11

The window box rarely is without a peeking child.

One observer suggested that maybe it was time to go out and bring more aphids in for the praying mantises. All agreed, and right after snack, with collection bags in tow, they went to forage for more aphids.

Once the mantises have hatched, resupply them with aphids regularly.

Day 32

Today provided a new lesson about the growth and development of the praying mantis. A few insects were hanging upside down from twigs of the big branch. "Are they sick? Are they dead?" children asked. Soon the mantises were encased in a clear sack. Beth assured the children that they were not dead, they were molting and showed them she could see a little bit of movement.

Day 34

While the mantises stayed in their growing sack, Beth started a discussion about how we grow and where our bones or skeletons are. "Feel your backbone, feel your bones inside your arm. That's your skeleton." She used a cricket specimen (dead and preserved for classroom teaching) to talk about the exoskeleton, the hard outside shell of the insect. She told the children that when an insect gets too big, it keeps still and grows another larger outside skeleton.

It wasn't long before the first praying mantis emerged from its "growing sack" and revealed a larger, slightly different version with a slight change in color. Beth retrieved the exoskeleton (outside molt) and left it on display for the children to explore.

The mantises prepare to molt. The molting process allows the mantis to shed its outside skeleton to make room for its enlarging body. The clear case protects the mantis body during this change while the new larger exoskeleton hardens. With each molt, the mantis emerges not only larger, but darker in color. Some species become darker brown with green areas on their legs while others, in adult stage, are entirely bright green.

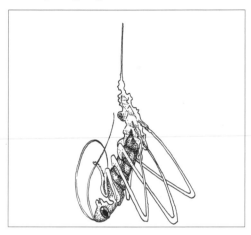

Prepare children for changes in mantises by discussing their own bodies and skeletons. Be sure children understand that, unlike insects' exoskeletons, our bones grow with us, so people don't have to molt.

Let children explore and feel the moltings.

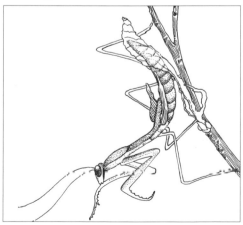

The mantises are now ready to eat a more varied diet.

Day 35

In reviewing the references in class Beth and the children discovered that the bigger praying mantis (which they now had) ate more than aphids. They ate flies and crickets. Flies were caught whenever possible and donated to the mantises. Beth brought crickets from the pet store as well.

Day 37

10 healthy mantises were left in the box. Rebecca told Beth that she was sure the insects didn't want to be in the nature box, they wanted to look around outside. Beth pointed out that we can't know how insects feel but that it was time to think about putting some of the mantises into a more natural environment. In a discussion, the class decided that the next day two of the praying mantises would move outside. But where? The children agreed to move them to the orange tree where there was lots of food.

Some of the mantises can be released.

Involve the children in deciding what happens to the insects in their projects. Creating situations in which children can make meaningful decisions is central to developmentally appropriate practice. This is a good time to point out how mantises help us by eating the aphids that can harm the plants we love. Many children—and adults—think of all insects as pests. But, as we understand them better, we see that many are beneficial.

Day 38

After a brief review of what was going to happen, the children watched Rebecca and Beth transfer 2 praying mantises into a portable jar by using an aphid leaf and a gentle hand.

Beth put the mantises on her hand and then transferred them to a few other children's hands so they could touch the insects. They felt the strength of the spindly-looking legs.

The children watched while Beth opened the lid and released the praying mantises into the orange tree.

The mantises blended in so well the children almost couldn't see them. "Oh there he is." Beth talked to the children about camouflage. Looking like the leaves makes it harder for birds and other predators to find them.

If you decide to free the insects, include children in the transfer to outside environment.

Carefully place the mantises you will be freeing in a glass jar. Be sure the jar's lid has holes.

If you are comfortable putting the insects on your hand, let the children touch them gently to see how they feel.

Release a few insects and observe them.

Notice how hard they are to see against the leaves and discuss camouflage.

Day 55

Over the last 2 weeks of the project, the mantises continued to molt. Today, the last molt occurred, and the praying mantis emerged with bright green wings.

It was time to release the remaining mantises. The children discussed where they should let them go.

When the last mantis has finished molting, prepare to release them.

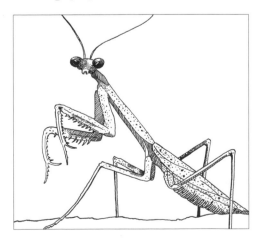

Day 56

The children spent the day discovering the praying mantis by touch, with Beth supervising. This was the last opportunity to observe the insect close-up because it would be difficult to catch outside.

Take a last opportunity to observe and touch the insects.

Day 57

The class walked across the yard to the tree they had chosen as the praying mantises' new home. Beth took the lid off the box and released the last insect into its new habitat.

Release the remaining praying mantises.

Gregory noticed that a bird flew close to one of the praying mantises to try to eat it. "The praying mantis got away," he said. "It's a good thing he had wings!"

This brings yet another relationship to other animals when you discuss how birds eat insects.

Field Trips

Take your children on field trips that help you and them discover insects in general. Finding a praying mantis would add a connection to the indoor mini-habitat study, but it may be hard to find a specific insect on any given trip. Enjoy an insect search in the neighborhood. Look under leaves, at the base of plants, and under rocks, as well as the topside of plants. Nature centers, botanical gardens, arboretums, zoos, and even nurseries have wonderful habitats for familiar and mysterious insects. Some of these places may have insect displays with real specimens and information on the connections between plants and animals.

These field trips can also provide a chance to release a few of the praying mantises in a friendly setting. If you release the young mantis on an earlier trip, organize a second or third field trip at a later date in hopes of finding a more mature mantis. Most likely, the caretakers of these settings will be happy to receive your praying mantis, but always check before releasing any animal into a new habitat.

Reference Books

Backyard Hunter —The Praying Mantis by Bianca Lavies, E.P. Dutton, 1990.

Insects Do the Strangest Things by Lenora and Arthur Hornblow, Random House Press, 1990.

Looking at Insects by David Suzuki, Warner Books, 1987.

Peterson Field Guides—Insects by Donald J. Borror, Houghton Mifflin Company, 1970.

Pets in a Jar by Seymour Simon, Penguin Books, 1982.

Resources

BioQuip
17803 La Salle Avenue
Gardena, CA 90248
(310-324-0620)
(310-324-7931) FAX

Insect Lore Products
P.O. Box 1535
Shafter, CA 93263
(800 Live Bug)
(805 746-6047)

Contact this nature supply company for information on obtaining animal species, support materials, and books.

Acorn Naturalists
17300 East 17th Street #J-236
Tustin, CA 92680
(800-422-8886)
(800-452-2802) FAX

Silver Burdett Press (Stopwatch Series)
P.O. Box 2649
Columbus, OH 43216
(800-848-9500)

Poems

"Mrs. Praying Mantis" from *A Hippopotamusn't and Other Animal Verses*, by J. Patrick Lewis, Dial, 1990.

Silkworms

INTRODUCTION

When we brought silkworms—actually silkworm caterpillars—into Beth's classroom, we were not prepared for the delight and enthusiasm they created with the children. At first, these insects are tiny, immobile pinpoints, not unlike poppy seeds. Then an astonishing process unfolds. It seems that almost from nothing, something alive appears and bores tiny holes in a mulberry leaf. From motionless black eggs, through the metamorphosis to silkmoths, to the final stage of egg laying and death, it is a miraculous adventure that takes place in a shoe box, on a table, in your classroom.

Much learning came out of the silkworm observations. Children learned about food acquisition, the connection between plants and insects, and important concepts about growth, development, and life cycle.

Beth enhances the children's experience by supplying the right materials at the right times. Magnifiers are useful early on, when the eggs are small and the worms are just developing. Later, the charts and reference books play an important role in helping children understand the full life cycle. Beth also weaves dramatic play, language, and artistic expression into the experience to enhance children's understanding.

HOW DO I BEGIN?

The first step in creating a silkworm habitat is to check the supply of local mulberry trees. Mulberry leaves are the only food source for these soon-to-be ravenous creatures. In late winter, locate a mulberry tree source. Early to mid-spring is a good time to get your silkworm eggs.

You can obtain silkworm eggs from a nature supply company (see references at the end of this chapter) or use eggs donated by another teacher from a previous silkworm habitat. Place the eggs on mulberry leaves in a box and your habitat is ready.

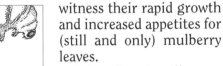

As the silkworm caterpillars hatch from and eat their eggs, you and your children will, like Beth's class, witness their rapid growth and increased appetites for (still and only) mulberry leaves.

When the caterpillars are done growing and eating, they will find a still place (often a corner of their box habitat) to spin their cocoons. ***IMPORTANT***: The silkworms need to be left untouched during this period. They will not successfully spin their cocoons if they are disturbed.

As more and more silkworm caterpillars progress to this cocoon stage, discuss the expected change. Use the images in reference books to see what is to come.

Silkmoths emerging from the silk cocoons are a delight to all. Tiny, yellow eggs soon follow to bring the life of the silkworm full cycle. Through the narrative on silkworms, notice how Beth provides an environment in her class that allows for children to explore the silkworms at different stages and in many different ways.

The common growth and development stages for silkworms follow this approximate timeline:

- Eggs incubate within 7 to 14 days.

- The larval stage (silkworm caterpillar) occurs between 25 and 30 days. The larval stage consists of five molting periods with alternating periods of eating and inactivity. The first 3 molts require 2 to 3 days of eating and approximately 1 to 1-1/2 days of inactivity before the molting is completed. The fourth molt requires 4 days of eating and 2 days of molting. The fifth molt requires 8 days of eating and then enters the pupal stage.

- The spinning of the cocoon takes three to four days.

- The pupal stage takes 10 to 14 days.

- The moth stage lasts 7 days, when mating and egg laying occur.

CREATING THE ENVIRONMENT

Silkworms are an easy springtime project for your classroom as long as you have a supply of mulberry leaves. Since mulberries are deciduous, you cannot start until the trees begin to leaf out. If you live in a cold climate and you're not in a year-round schedule, check carefully to be sure you have enough time between when the leaves are available and when your program ends.

To create the silkworm mini-habitat, you will need:

Silkworm Eggs
Obtain these from a biosupply company the first year. (At the end of the section, we'll give you instructions for harvesting and storing the eggs yourself.)

Mulberry Leaves
You will need a continuous supply of fresh leaves. Locate nearby trees (they are fairly common). This is a good opportunity to enlist the help of parents and local residents. You will be amazed at how much the silkworms can eat once they get near full size. If you wrap the leaves in damp paper towels and put them in a plastic bag, you can store the leaves in the refrigerator for a few days. Silkworms are sensitive to pesticides. If you think the leaves have been sprayed, wash and wipe them before placing the silkworms on them.

Shoe Box
Use a standard shoe box or medium carton. For better viewing, cut out the sides and replace them with a see-through material. You can do the same thing with the top, but make holes for ventilation. You may want to use a screening material for the lid. Set the box in a place where the silkworms will not be exposed to direct sunlight.

Reference Materials

Put out information about silkworms near the new mini-habitat. See the end of this chapter for suggestions.

BETH'S SILKWORM EXPERIENCE

The Story

Spring had arrived, and the mulberry trees in the play yard near Beth's school were beginning to reveal good green growth. These mulberry leaves are the silkworm's only food. Beth knew it was time to order the silkworm eggs from a catalog that specializes in nature study activities.

Steps and Teaching Tips

Find the mulberry trees in your area and wait until they are beginning to leaf before you start. Be sure you have a generous supply of leaves from a neighbor or friend.

Order silkworm eggs from a catalog (see the end of the chapter for references). Use teacher networks and science centers as other sources for eggs.

Day 1

A few days after the eggs arrived, they began to lighten in color. Beth knew it was time to prepare the children for the new arrivals in the classroom.

Beth took the children on a nature walk through the play yard to visit the trees (now lush with big mid-spring leaves). As they examined the trees using all their senses, many talked about how the trees felt and smelled. As they lay in the shade of the mulberry tree, Beth listened to remarks and observations made by the children on who lives in trees and who eats leaves. Beth had packed along magnifiers and collection boxes for anything interesting they might discover. Cassie asked to bring a leaf inside to add to the leaf display in the classroom.

The outdoor experience prior to introducing the silkworm eggs will begin to establish connections between the new mini-habitat and outdoor setting.

Experience the setting using all the senses.

Magnifiers and books are great for enhancing outdoor learning.

Familiarize children with things like leaves. Bring the outdoors in.

Day 2

Before the children arrived, Beth made a bed from a single, large mulberry leaf and laid it in a shoe box with 10 tiny silkworm eggs resting on top of it. She replaced the lid in which she had cut and screened a window. Once the children arrived, she sat the box next to her while she talked with a group of children who were cutting out pictures from magazines. There were many pictures of insects, even caterpillars.

It didn't take long for the children to notice Beth's box. Jasmine peered through the screened window on the lid of the box and whispered, "What's in here?" Beth made suggestions in a similar whisper that conveyed not only mystery, but also that a gentle approach should be taken with the contents of this new habitat. With a closer look, Jamie recognized the leaf from the mulberry tree outside and brought over the one from the leaf table. Rodney noticed the dark gray specks, which he called dirt.

Joanne picked up the reference book on silkworms, pointed to an enlarged photo of silkworm eggs and said that this leaf had sand on it, too. At this point, Beth looked at the book with the children and read to them that the little specks were eggs, silkworm caterpillar eggs. They sure didn't look like any eggs anyone there had seen.

Throughout the day, many children checked the box and browsed through the books. That afternoon, Adam noticed that the eggs had changed color a little bit. Everyone was anxious to see what was going to come out of these tiny eggs.

Before introduction, prepare the environment with good viewing windows.

Magazine picture cuttings for nature books can lead an activity. Looking at pictures allows children additional opportunities to become familiar with animals they are about to study.

Note how Beth creates the opportunity and then allows the children the pleasure of discovery.

The children form their ideas through observation and then use the references for additional information.

Day 3

The silkworm eggs were definitely one of the major attractions of the day. The children checked them frequently so they could assess any changes. This gave Beth a chance to restate the need for gentleness, which meant no touching while the insects were so small.

The children further explored the books on silkworms. The pictures of the caterpillars brought children together to discuss the insects' gray-green color; to count their legs; to note how they cling to and eat leaves; and to laugh at the funny bumps on their back. These and many other observations, small and large, served to bring the silkworms shown in books into the children's world.

As children overcome their fear of insects, they have a great natural desire to handle them. This is a good opportunity to teach about observing the natural world without disturbing it.

Bringing the insects and the references together stimulates observation and conversation. Try to write down the children's words. Post them if possible.

Day 4

Something amazing started to happen. Where yesterday there had been small eggs on a fresh mulberry leaf, there were now tiny wiggly stringlike creatures crawling on a leaf with little holes in it. Apparently, the eggs had hatched, and according to Chelsea, "The worms

As silkworms grow, more children will become involved with the habitat; and with their enthusiasm parents and

came out!" By the end of the day, Beth's children had brought in children from other classes and unsuspecting parents to share the miraculous event.

siblings will be drawn to share the excitement.

Add one fresh leaf when the silkworms hatch.

Day 8

Over the last few days, the children explored the big picture reference books. They compared the information from the books to the small silkworms. The two big leaves had kept the insects well fed. But now the tiny worms had eaten much of the leaves, and what was left was looking dry. Jennifer expressed her concern that the "poor silkworms need more food."

Allow children to recognize the need for more food.

The outside adventure that followed allowed the children to explore the mulberry tree with a new appreciation for its function and importance for insects. As they looked for outdoor relatives to their shoe box silkworms, they found not silkworms, but ladybugs. The class brought a few leaves inside and all watched the silkworm caterpillars vigorously consume their fresh moist meal of mulberry leaves.

Let the children lead you to the food source. If mulberry trees are nearby, take advantage of the opportunity to explore them.

Since silkworms are not part of the natural environment, you must help build connections between trees and other insects. Search for new insects who also use the tree for food and protection.

Day 10

Since the silkworms are hardier and have grown to almost an inch, Beth decided to take them outside the shoe box. She made a large bed of mulberry leaves on the table and gently set five silkworms on the leaves. This provided the children with a much better view of the caterpillars' movements. To ensure that the silkworms were not harmed, Beth taught the one-finger technique of gently touching the insects. She provided magnifiers so the children could get close enough to examine all the details of texture, shape, and color, and share and gain language to express what they observed.

Here again is an opportunity to stress careful handling and observation techniques.

If you use a microscope, keep the silkworm's exposure short. Silkworms are very sensitive to light as well as to loud noises.

Later that day, to expand on the investigation, Beth enlisted a parent to help the children examine the silkworms under a microscope that was on temporary loan to the school. This observation required a one-to-one format because children needed guidance focusing and taking care not to leave the silkworm in the intense light of the scope.

Opportunities to use scopes or large stationary magnifiers may not always avail themselves, but when they do Beth grabs them. The children were amazed when they looked through the microscope and saw a monstrous gray-green creature wiggle about. The new perspective brought a renewed interest and enthusiasm in looking at silkworms. Feelings of fear and apprehension of these and other insects can be eased as children see themselves in a more powerful and responsible position as gentle caretakers.

Teaching in developmentally appropriate ways can be very labor-intensive. Parents can be helpful. Here a parent works the microscope. Parents can also work at tables where care with the insects is necessary. They can also write down children's comments.

Notice how Beth takes good advantage of an opportunity that arises by bringing out the microscope and clearing an area for viewing. This is not a shot in the dark, though. She knows that one of her goals is to give children lots of opportunities to observe the silkworms and discuss their observations. So it's easy for this activity to emerge in the moment.

Day 13

More leaves must be harvested. Hardly a day goes by without a need to replace the top single layer of leaves that cover the worms with cool moisture. The children cover the 1-1/2 inch long caterpillars with the leaves, and watch them crawl to the top, munching all the way.

Keep silkworm caterpillars moist and well fed with fresh mulberry leaves. Leaves and silkworms dry out quickly.

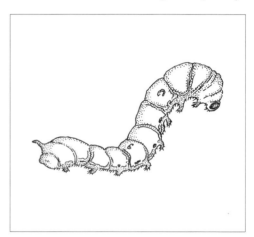

Day 15

Some of the children engaged in dramatic play and became worms. They wiggled along the floor munching on invisible mulberry leaves. Some pretended they were babies hatching. Some relived the magnifier experience from the silkworms' perspective. "Can you see my bumpy cracked back?"

Dramatic play is one of the important ways children develop their understandings of the world.

On day 15, the dramatic play was spontaneous. Here, Beth picks up the children's interest and facilitates their play by providing materials that encourage it.

Day 16

Beth brought in old socks. On the hands and arms of preschoolers, they became silkworms, wriggling around the room and crawling up the mulberry trees in the yard.

Day 22

The silkworm caterpillars had begun to slow down in their eating. One had even crawled up into the corner of the box and was very still. Some thought it was sick. Cody was sure it had eaten too much and just needed to rest its tummy.

Encourage children to come up with their own theories on what is happening in the mini-habitat. Then, as developments occur, they can test and revise their theories.

Day 23

The silkworm that had stayed in a corner so still now had white threads all around it. The book said it was spinning a cocoon. The children remembered another mini-habitat where caterpillars had made their houses (chrysalises) and had emerged as butterflies. What would these look like? The books revealed a possibility...the silkmoth.

Using the children's interest in the reference books and children's stories, guide them to their own discovery. Try to tie in other nature experiences. This adds continuity and a base for reference. The butterfly life cycle, for example, is similar to the silkmoth's cycle.

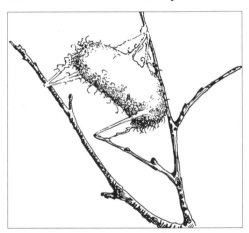

Day 24

Beth hung pictures of silkmoths on the wall above the shoe box habitat. Each day brought more and more silk-threaded cocoons. Each day saw more and more children coming to the box to count the cocoons and to see who was left.

Day 29

Beth posted a completed sequence chart next to the moth photographs.

The dramatic play seemed focused on becoming cocoons and there was much talk of growing and changing.

Sequence charts depicting the stages of silkworm metamorphosis can be helpful if they are of good size, simple, and well defined.

Day 34

This morning in the box, the children discovered a light tan insect with brown wings. The silkmoths had emerged. There was great excitement as the children observed the moths and compared them with the charts and with other flying insects they knew.

Increasingly, children will find meaning in symbolic displays.

Emergence of the silkmoth will generate a wave of excitement, whether the children's expectations are confirmed, or whether they are amazed by the unanticipated. This is a great time to listen to words and write them down. You could turn their comments into a letter that children illustrate and take home.

Day 36

Today, the silkmoths' full cycle was visibly completed as the children watched the newly-hatched silkmoths mate and lay spreads of bright yellow eggs on the leaves and walls of their habitat.

Go outside, revisit the trees (leaves) where this project started, find some moths or butterflies, and reread a story about metamorphoses.

Day 39

Within a few days after laying the eggs, the moths died. Everyone seemed to accept that this is how this insect lives its life.

Beth decided to hold off on talking about the uses people have for the silk cocoon. After all, the cocoon will be available long after the last silkmoth has died. Beth and her class reviewed the growth chart, explored the moths in the display, and reminisced over the photos to recall events of the last few weeks.

As the moths die, review and discuss their full life cycle. They have done their work, spinning their silk and laying eggs for the next generation. If you have a compost pile, add the dead moths to it to emphasize another part of the cycle, how things that die can nourish the soil, helping plants grow, which we and insects can use for food.

Day 40

The yellow eggs that had been laid on the side of the box began to turn grayish-black, not unlike poppy seeds. Did these eggs look familiar to anyone? Stephen remembered the little black specks on the leaf when the silkworm habitat first came into the classroom.

As the eggs harden, we are back at the beginning. For next year's silkworms, cut the shoe box into platforms with the various areas that contain eggs. Put them in a well-sealed, plastic container and refrigerate them until next spring when the mulberry leaves are again plentiful. You will likely have more than you need for next year's class, so share some with a fellow teacher.

Cocoons should be left out and discussed. Bring in something made of silk for children to see and touch.

Field Trips

Take your children places where they can investigate many different types of insects, especially caterpillars. If you find a park or neighborhood location that has become home for butterflies or moth caterpillars, take periodic trips there to see the growth and development of these insects that are related to the silkworm. If fruited mulberry trees are nearby, you may even find silkworms.

You can find displays and information on butterflies and moths at natural history museums, arboretums, and botanical gardens. The beautiful and diverse plants surrounding these settings provide wonderful opportunities to see caterpillars and, almost always, butterflies. Insect houses and educational displays are often in zoos and nature centers. A community Japanese garden or cultural center may have a display on the traditional silk industry that depends on the silkworm.

Reference Books

Butterflies and Moths by Rosamund Cox and Barbara Cork, Usborne Publishing Limited, 1990.

Discovering Butterflies and Moths by Keith Porter, Bookwright Press, 1990.

Silkworms by Sylvia A. Johnson, Lerner Publishing, 1982.

Keeping Minibeasts—Caterpillars by Barrie Watts, Franklin Watts, 1989.

Resources

Insect Lore Products
P.O. Box 1535
Shafter, CA 93263
(805 746-6047)
(800 Live Bug)

BioQuip
17803 La Salle Avenue
Gardena, CA 90248
(310 324-0620)
(310 324-7931) FAX

Acorn Naturalists
17300 East 17th Street #J-236
Tustin, CA 92680
(800-422-8886)
(800-452-2802) FAX

Silver Burdett Press (Stopwatch Series)
P.O. Box 2649
Columbus, OH 43216
(800-848-9500)

Snails

INTRODUCTION

Snails are, for young children, one of the most delightful creatures to find their way into a mini- habitat. Snails are relatively rugged, and children will be able to explore these one-footed creatures with a hands-on approach. After a few spritzes of water to awaken the resting (estivating) adult snails, you can lift them from their green, leafy bed to a tabletop for investigation. The children will get a close view of the snail's two sets of tentacles moving in and out, gathering information about its new environment. Feeling the soft and slimy foot on an arm, or discovering the hard shell with a gentle finger touch gives the child tactile information, which makes the snail study meaningful. Watching the snail make a slime trail (see activity below), munch on geranium leaves, or protect itself by retreating into its shell provides many opportunities for your small children to share with each other and their parents. If time allows, study the snails for a couple of months. You and your class may observe egg laying and the development of tiny transparent little snails, bringing wonderful lessons on growth and change in nature.

HOW DO I BEGIN?

Starting a snail habitat is as easy as an early morning visit to your front yard. Give your outside plants and lawn a thorough watering in the evening before bed, and by early morning, you may find a good supply of snails crawling along porch steps, walkways, flower bed borders or under big, leafy plants.

If your home is snailless, talk to your friends or neighbors who are gardeners. They will undoubtedly be happy to donate as many of these normally pesky creatures as they have. *Just make sure that no poison has been used in their (or your) garden.*

Gently, pick up the snails by the shell with an index finger and thumb lift. Set them in a container. Use a sturdy plastic container like the clear, reusable ones from a bakery or restaurant. Make sure the container is waterproof, because your snails need a somewhat moist environment.

Include some plants from the snail's natural home, especially the plants you may have found the snail living on at the time.

When the children meet the snails in the classroom, a clear-sided container will allow many to view long before they are ready to touch. For those who *are* ready to explore further, place one or two snails in front of each child while modeling the simple two-finger lift approach.

Remember to leave reference books out with the snails. The easy access to books helps children to use them to understand what they are seeing and to learn about what they may see next. It connects books with learning.

As you read the narrative about Sue's class, note how she listens to the children's words while they explore these new creatures. The children's discussion of motion, direction, and color strengthen important language and social skills. You will also see how Sue and the snails share a wonderful art project with the children.

You will most likely start with snails in varying stages of development, but since you may eventually discover eggs, our overview of snail development begins at the egg stage. Following is a growth timeline for most common garden snails, but allow for variations dependent on the species.

Snails:

- Eggs are laid 1 month after mating. Snails prefer to lay their eggs in soil or on a soft leafy area.

- The incubation period occurs during the second and fourth weeks. Clear baby snails hatch from their milky white eggs.

- The shell darkens and hardens after 1 month.

- Snails develop whorls on the shell as they grow larger and larger in the following months. A fully grown snail has 4 to 5 whorls.

- Adult snails are not able to mate and reproduce until after their third year.

Remember, snails will go into periods of hibernation (cold weather) and estivation (hot weather) depending on the availability of food and the weather conditions present.

CREATING THE ENVIRONMENT

The best way to gather snails is to look in your yard or ask your neighbors if they have snails they will be happy to share. ***IMPORTANT:*** Make sure no one has spread poison on the snails. This would not be safe for the children.

To create the snail mini-habitat, you will need:

Container
A clear-sided plastic container, the size of a shoe box or larger, will allow maximum visibility and portability.

Food Source
Keep the container filled with green, leafy plants. Start with the plants you found near the snails and then use children's suggestions. Have a spray-bottle handy to help keep snails moist. Optional: sprinkle limestone powder to give the snails the calcium they need to build their shells.

Reference Materials
As with all habitats, keep books, charts, posters, magnifiers, and puppets available. Also provide music and literature on snails and creatures that live under plants and in the soil. If empty shells from dead snails are available, leave them on the table for investigation.

Suggestions for facilitating this project:

1. After you have done a "presearch" for likely areas of snail colonies, take your children on a local field trip to gather snails (with magnifiers available). This allows them to exercise

their natural investigative nature and to see where they can find snails when they are away from your site. Investigate the other animals (insects and worms) that live with the snails.

2. A great art project that reveals how snails move involves a large piece of butcher paper, tape, vegetable dye food coloring, and a few snails. Place the butcher paper across a long table and tape it in place. Dot the paper with small drops of food dye. Ask the children to pick up the snails from the box and lay them foot side down on the dye. As the snails move, they will pick up the dye and make a colorful trail. This creates a lovely and unusual art project with lessons in color and color mixing as snails cross over many colors in their path. It also allows children to more closely see the slime trail the snail needs to move; they can also track the movements of each snail.

3. Snails may be unattractive to adults and children entering a class after the project has started (or who are reserved from the beginning). Children securely handling these small creatures sends an invitation to others to come and see the fun. Peer relationships and language development flourish as they share their excitement. Bring uninvolved children near to slowly share with the involved children. Encouraging song and poetry started by you and finished by the children will provide each child with his or her own avenue of access to the project.

THE SNAILS IN SUE'S CLASS

The Story

Steps and Teaching Tips

Day 1

It was a crisp, somewhat overcast fall morning when Sue packed up the small clear plastic containers (her creature boxes), magnifiers, netted insect boxes, and a couple of small books to take along on a "discovery walk" of the small schoolyard. This regular Monday morning tradition found her group of three- and four-year-old nature

Take the lead by gathering your own supplies with some enthusiasm. Your increasingly interested group will catch on and follow eagerly.

enthusiasts prepared with their own collection boxes and the anticipation of visiting old friends in the garden. The insects found near their school building have become a comfortable part of their play and their learning.

As they start their walk, the children share their recollections of past explorations with songs and stories. They sing about worms in the soil and ladybugs that help the hollyhocks grow tall and healthy. As Sue and her group pass the small garden, Mariana, using a grasshopper puppet, talks about the praying mantis' home in the squash patch. She remembers the good work the mantises did last summer as they protected the squash by eating the aphids.

At the back fence, Sue began to look through the geranium leaves on the ground for sowbugs. Following her lead, child after child examined the underside of the leaves and the base of the large plants nearby, finding not only the sowbugs, but ladybugs, worms, and ants.

Michael, staying close to Sue, made the discovery she had hoped someone would. He found what he announced as a "nail" pointing to a creature which had retreated into its protective shell. Sue examined the discovery and announced to everyone, "Look, Michael has found a snail. Maybe we can bring the snail out so we can get a better look." Michael was hesitant to remove the snail from its firm hold on the geranium, so Sue demonstrated a gentle technique to lift it by its shell. She slipped it into the clear container. "He's hiding," D. J. said as he moved the clear-sided container up and down, trying to get a glimpse of the creature.

As the snail stayed hidden, interest dwindled and only a couple of children remained. Others went in search of more active subjects. Suddenly, there came excited sounds from one of the snail examiners, "He's coming out, he's coming out! Look he has horns."

Questions and observations rang out. "How does it find its way in its new home? What was it looking for?"

Once is rarely enough for discovery of any one location. Explore and re-explore your surrounding environment.

Nature study is not an isolated activity you place on the science table. It can be a continuous part of your children's daily learning: a way of learning.

Encourage the expression of past experience with poetry and song. They are connectors of past and new experience. Children don't always have to be quiet to study nature.

Using puppets allows a wonderful medium to express past learning and increase recall for the whole group. Your puppets belong outside as well as in.

Entice your children into discovery by demonstration and example. Look for things you are sure you can find. It adds to the success and leads to their continued exploration. A "presearch" before the children arrive can help.

Someone suggested that the snail was hungry. Someone else recommended putting a leaf (like the one he was found on) in the box with him.

Sue listened and contributed correct terminology and information in small doses. Sue said that, yes, the horns are like feelers; she gave them the correct name, tentacles. She confirmed the childrens' hypotheses that the snail used them like eyes and a nose to help it find its way in its new home. Sue asked Michael where he had found the snail. "Michael, did you find the snail on a geranium plant?" With this clue, a search for the geranium leaves began, and with it, the additional discovery of several other snails.

Bring to other children the discoveries being made and invite children to examine them. They will likely continue their own search.

Allow all explorers to share their knowledge and information. Encourage resident experts.

Not all children will be engaged at the same level. With peer excitement and modeling, more and more children will become involved.

You can facilitate the discovery by giving correct information while validating the children's statements. As the discussion continues, add what you know. When you get to something you don't know, tell the children you can look it up when you get back inside.

Lead them to their own discovery.

Day 2

Once inside the classroom, the snails became the subject of several joyful discussions throughout the day. Jennifer closely examined the broad jellylike "foot" of one of the snails as it carried itself and its home atop this strong muscle. Through her firsthand experience, she connected with the story Sue read this morning. The story had lead to a discussion about how a snail is protected by its shell.

Melissa flipped through a book on small ground roving creatures and recalled Devon saying that he wore a jacket today to keep himself warm and that the snail wears a shell to keep itself warm, too. Devon's jacket became a shell in dramatic play later that day.

Jackye put her two index fingers on her forehead and pretended she had tentacles like the snails. For most of the days ahead there were discussions on the senses—human senses and snail senses.

Having reference materials near the mini-habitat display and reading age appropriate nonfiction books that show the animals in the pictures and discuss them in the text, brings more meaning to what the children see in the habitat.

As children explore nature around them, bring relevance to their lives by pointing out the connections between us and their friends in the habitat. Exploring senses is a great way to do that.

Day 3

This morning brought interested children to an early reinvestigation of the snails mini-habitat. Sue needed little encouragement to bring the portable snail habitat outside. She placed the snails on a shady table, and they became the subject of much inquiry and discussion.

As Michael explained what he had learned to a child who had not yet been drawn into the snail study, A. J. noticed that the snails had eaten the leaves from the first day and that the leaves were drying out a bit. The group foraged for more geranium leaves so the snails could have lunch. As the children explored the snails' natural environment, other snails appeared and were added to the mini-habitat.

Bring your habitats outside whenever possible. It brings nature study outside where the possibilities are endless. It helps make connections between the habitat and real nature as well as brings interested children from other classes in to learn and be taught by your resident experts.

Day 4

The count of found snails was steadily rising (the latest number was seven). Sue thought a more meaningful hands-on experience could develop if she brought in a few snails from her home garden and some from an organic gardening neighbor. The increased number would provide each child with at least 1 or 2 to explore, allowing their investigation to unfold. Now, with enough snails to go around, the stage was set for more exploration.

This morning when the snail mini-habitat was brought to the shaded outside table and after the leaves were gathered, Sue suggested that they make a bed out of leaves on the table. Both the classroom snails and the new arrivals were gently lifted from their viewing boxes and laid on the table for further exploration. Sue watched the snails being removed with care. She explained about the snails being found near her home to open the conversation to any other recollections of such findings the children might have had. Sure enough someone remembered snails crawling along their walkway at home when it rained. "Do snails come out in the rain?" Sue inquired. Many thought they did. So with a suggestion that "we could make it rain on the snails," Sue pulled out the water spritzer and the rain fell, bringing out a few snails. Now the children had one more piece of information to help them recreate a healthy snail mini-habitat environment.

Use your resources. Remember to be very sure no poison has been used on the snails you bring to your class.

Hands-on exploration is the most meaningful way your children learn. Each will come to snails at his or her own pace. Again, peer modeling is your greatest tool. You need to be there to maintain a safe environment for the children and snails and to demonstrate gentleness with the animals.

Bring in home and family experiences to assist your children in making connections about nature.

Let them find their own solutions whenever possible.

Day 5

The past 2 days had provided many opportunities to bring the snails out of their containers. During these times, Sue observed the children become more comfortable. She saw their hesitancy replaced with a joyful acceptance of the snails crawling on their shirt sleeves and hanging "surefooted" from their hands. Cautioning the children to handle with care, Sue cupped her hands inches beneath a hanging snail so all could test the strength of the snail's single foot without risking injury to it.

Again, comfort with snails will be quick for some and take awhile for others.

Be there for guidance and support.

Day 6

Sue kept the majority of the snail family in 1 clear plastic shoe box full of moist green leaves. But last night, she had left just a few snails with a minimum of leaf matter in a container covered with black paper. She expected this would keep the container dark and cool and encourage the snails to take a trip on the walls of the container.

Preplanning a discovery can keep the wonder in the experience.

Today, the paper was removed to the delight of those watching the great view of a yellowish snail foot plodding across the side of the clear plastic wall. David noticed the slime trail that was left as the snail moved on its journey. Sue explained that the "slime" helps the snail move and some is left behind in silvery streaks. Children then took more notice of the direction of the snails' travel. Words and phrases like "came from," "going to," "wiggly line," "short trail," and "long trail," came from the observers. A great deal was talked about, thought about, and acted out as the subject of how creatures, especially snails, move proved to be an interesting part of this habitat study.

A good lesson in direction.

Listen and help with the sharing of language as the children strive to share their excitement and discovery.

Day 8

The discovery and discussion about snail trails yesterday led into an art activity. As her group sat down for snail discovery, Sue provided a white butcher paper surface on a long table. Each child had a separate sheet labeled with his or her name when they sat down. As the children took the snails out of the shoe box, Sue put a drop of food coloring on the paper in front of each child. She suggested that each put a snail on the drop and see what happens. Sue and the children witnessed a wonderful art project emerge as colorful streams were left on the papers when each snail picked up a bit of the dye on its foot and made one-of-a-kind "snail paintings."

An art activity that brings together color, movement, and snail behavior comes from a previous day's discovery about snail trails.

(When setting up this activity, alternate colors from child to child.)

Sue renewed yesterday's discussion by pointing out the long trail left by Matthew's snail. Along with conversation on going up and down and straight and curvy, something else arose. As the snails crossed each other's paths, the dyes blended and a lesson of color mixing began as Ricardo said "Look, my snail made orange." Others shared their observations about the colored streams. Sue chimed in with excited anticipation as she said, "Oh, look! Eric's snail is moving his blue foot over near Mariana's snail's yellow stream." Everyone

Your enthusiasm can help children to their own discovery.

became attentive to the event. "What happened?" Sue asked. "They made green like his geranium leaves!" Michael answered.

Day 9

Yesterday, Sue recorded the children's words with a small tape recorder. When the children came in this morning, they discovered their snail paintings on the walls with a few of their words printed at the bottom of each paper. Sue read their comments as each requested them. The recall of the art project was powerful as many of the children explored their snail paintings with finger tips tracing the tracks as their words were shared and conversation expanded.

When afternoon pickup time came, the children dragged their parents to the snail table to learn about the snails and to view the paintings that covered the wall. The parents were amazed at the beautiful art and somewhat surprised with the delight their children had with snails...of all things.

Use a tape recorder or an assistant to help document the words children use to explain their discovery.

Let children see their words with the pictures.

Sue is lucky because most parents come to the class daily to drop off and pick up their children. You can also share the children's mini-habitat experiences in written form with parents. Parents become involved because children are so enthusiastic.

Day 12

The children talked, sang, and made poems about how the snails move slowly on their one foot. The room became full of child-sized snails roaming around the classroom retreating within their shells when they perceived danger. Sue had started one such occurrence when she noticed Lenny curled up in a ball as he slipped on his shoe after nap. She commented on how he looked like a snail curling up in its shell. Well, as often happens, the play took off and imaginary snail trails appeared. Most everyone could see the giant imaginary geranium leaves.

At the beginning of dramatic play, get involved. See where the children take it. Let them use it often; it helps in sharing recall with each other.

Day 15

With the increasing knowledge and comfort the children exhibited around the snails, Sue took opportunities to step back and photograph the children in their exploration. She photographed leaf foraging, snail painting, dramatic play episodes, and children playing or observing the snails in their mini-habitat. The pictures came back last night. But instead of making a poster at home she let the children look at the pictures and explain what was happening in each. Writing these comments down, she had provided a great recall experience.

When your budget allows, take photographs and give children a chance to recall and provide words to the event in the photograph.

Day 17

From all the observation and discussion of how snails move came an interest in the many ways animals move. With this came an exploration of body parts and movement.

With music accompaniment, Sue and her three- and four-year-olds became everything from single-footed snails to multilegged caterpillars.

Again, exploration of their own bodies and movement can be important connections to discussion of movements of animals.

Day 25

The snails spent more and more time encased in their sealed shells estivating. The children began to lose interest, and Sue knew it was time to return them to their environment. They took their snails out to a part of the school yard away from their garden and released them onto geraniums and other plants the children knew snails would eat.

However, the project was not over. Children continued to bring snails in from home, and in one case from the home of grandparents. Sue always made a place for the visiting snails in her classroom.

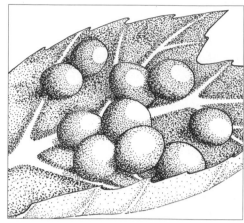

Sue decided that her children had gotten as much from the observations as they were likely to get. She knew that, if she waited until spring, the snails were likely to reproduce. If they were lucky, the children would get a chance to see the small white snail eggs just under ground level. Then, tiny, almost translucent snails would emerge and the next generation would begin.

Reference Books

Snails by Sylvia Johnson, Lerner Natural Science Book, 1982.

Keeping Minibeasts by Chris Henwood, Franklin Watts, 1988.

Snail—Stopwatch by Jens Olesen, Silver Burdett Press, 1988.

Life of the Snail by Theres Buholzer, Carolrhoda Books, 1984.

Stories

The Biggest House in the World by Leo Lionni, Pantheon, 1968.

The Guest by James Marshall, Houghton Mifflin, 1975.

Here Comes John by Bob Graham, Little, Brown, 1983.

Snails Spell by Joanne Ryder, Puffin Books, Penguin Books, 1988.

Poems

"Snail" from No One Writes a Letter to the Snail: Poems, by Maxine W. Kumin, Putnam, 1962.

"The Snail" by James Reeves, from These Small Stones: Poems, selected by Norma Farber and Myra Cohn Livingston, Harper Collins, 1987.

Resources

Insect Lore Products
P.O. Box 1535
Shafter, CA 93263
(805 746-6047)
(800 Live Bug)

BioQuip
17803 La Salle Avenue
Gardena, CA 90248
(310 324-0620)
(310 324-7931) FAX

Acorn Naturalists
17300 East 17th Street #J-236
Tustin, CA 92680
(800-422-8886)
(800-452-2802) FAX

Silver Burdett Press (Stopwatch Series)
P.O. Box 2649
Columbus, OH 43216
(800-848-9500)

Field Trips

Field trips for your snail study can be as easy and frequent as trips to the school garden or taking time during outside play to explore the yard's flowerbeds or overgrown areas near the fence. Neighborhood walks can give children special time to look under leaves and at the base of the plants along the sidewalk in an area just around the block. Carry this exploration a bit further and visit a local park, city garden, or arboretum. It is a good idea to contact the maintenance office of these places and find out if snail poisons have been used at these locations.

Other Mini-Habitats to Try

Butterflies

INTRODUCTION

This mini-habitat presents a wonderful opportunity to bring something indoors for a closer look that may have already enchanted your children. These beautiful flighty creatures are wonderful to watch in their natural environment, but so much more of their story can be revealed to small children when they are examined in a temporary and easily accessible mini-environment.

As these tiny insects grow from transparent microscopic caterpillars into visible, leaf-munching multileg creatures, your children will become increasingly involved in watching their behavior through the windows of this box habitat. The children will be enchanted as they observe the caterpillars grow in size, crawl out of their outside skeletons (3 or 4 times in their life cycle), and eventually become still, form a chrysalis, and hang around for a rest as they use this pupa stage to metamorphose into the familiar butterfly.

As you help them discover, through outdoor exploration, the connections between what they see in the box with the plants and insects outside, the natural environment becomes more important and meaningful to them and presents a world of endless new discoveries. From this project can come an experience that can be retold over and over through their words, song, and dramatic play as they relay the story of how the caterpillars turned to butterflies.

CREATING THE ENVIRONMENT

To create the caterpillar to butterfly mini-habitat, you will need:

Butterflies or Caterpillars
If you look very, very closely, you may find butterfly eggs on the underside of plant leaves in the school yard or in the park, but a more visible stage would be the caterpillar as spring begins to warm. If caterpillars are hard to find in a nearby outdoor environment, buy them through a nature or biology supply company (see the end of this chapter for more information), and you and your children will be able to watch caterpillars turn to butterflies any time of year. These companies commonly send out painted lady caterpillars. These are beautiful and colorful butterflies, but you may find equally wonderful local caterpillars to bring inside for your children to study in a mini-habitat. Be sure to include some of the leaves of the plant you found it on. Chances are it's a caterpillar favorite.

Shoe Box Container
Use a standard shoe box or medium carton. For better viewing, cut out the sides and replace them with a see-through material. You can do the same

thing with the top, but make holes for ventilation. You may want to use a screening material for the lid. Set the box in a place where the caterpillars will not be exposed to direct sunlight.

Food Source

You need only to add leaves and branches of the plants you found the caterpillars on. For commercially purchased caterpillars, use recommended leaves.

Reference Materials

Reference books, magnifiers, sequence charts, pictures laminated on table, posters with photos of children exploring insect puppets.

Suggestions for facilitating the caterpillar to butterfly mini-habitat:

1. Keep a small shoe box (clear plastic is best) on hand to bring the caterpillars a little closer to your young nature explorers. A week or 2 after hatching, bring a few sturdy caterpillars out to discover a new leaf bed in the box. Allow the children to view the caterpillars' muscle movements involved in eating and crawling. Supervise a gentle one-finger touch exploration so the children can experience the texture of these fascinating insects. Make sure that magnifiers are out on the table as the children investigate their crawling friends close at hand.

2. Bring your portable box of caterpillars outside to add opportunities for recall and to help the children make connections with their friends in the habitat and out-of-door environment. Make sure books and puppets follow you outside as they help children formulate and express their questions.

3. If there is no room in your budget for commercial caterpillar puppets and you just want a fun activity, bring in old socks. You and the children can dress them up with eyes and mouths or just leave them plain. As the children express their learning about how caterpillars eat and demonstrate how they crawl, they will be teaching their peers, recalling their experience, and finding a new medium to express their questions.

For all of these recommended activities, take photos during the activity and display them on a poster. Ask your children if they can tell you what is going on in each picture. Write down their words.

Reference Books

Butterflies, The World of Nature Series by John Farrand, Gallery Books, 1990.

Butterfly and Caterpillar by Barrie Watts, Silver Burdett Press, 1989.

Familiar Butterflies by Richard K. Walton, Audubon Pocket guides (reference), 1981.

Where Butterflies Grow (in story format) by Joanne Ryder, Lodestar Books, 1989.

Life of the Butterfly by Heidersoe and Andreas Fischer-Nagel, Carolrhoda Books, Inc., 1987.

Peterson First Guides—Caterpillars by Amy Bartlett Wright, Houghton Mifflin Company, 1993.

Peterson First Guide to Butterflies and Moths by Paul Opler, Houghton Mifflin Company, 1994.

Resources

Insect Lore Products
P.O. Box 1535
Shafter, CA 93263
(800 Live Bug)
(805 746-6047)

Contact this nature supply company for information on obtaining animal species, support materials, and books.

BioQuip
17803 La Salle Avenue
Gardena, CA 90248
(310 324-0620)
(310 324-7931) FAX

Acorn Naturalists
17300 East 17th Street #J-236
Tustin, CA 92680
(800-422-8886)
(800-452-2802) FAX

Silver Burdett Press (Stopwatch Series)
P.O. Box 2649
Columbus, OH 43216
(800-848-9500)

Stories

The Caterpillar and the Polliwog by Jack Kent, Prentice-Hall, 1982.

The Very Hungry Caterpillar by Eric Carle, Philomel, 1979.

Poems

"Caterpillars" by Aileen Fisher, from *Surprises,* selected by Lee Bennett Hopkins, Harper Collins, 1984.

"The Tickle Rhyme" by Ian Serraillier, from *Roger Was a Razor Fish and Other Poems,* compiled by Jill Bennett, Lothrop, Lee & Shepard, 1980.

Ladybugs

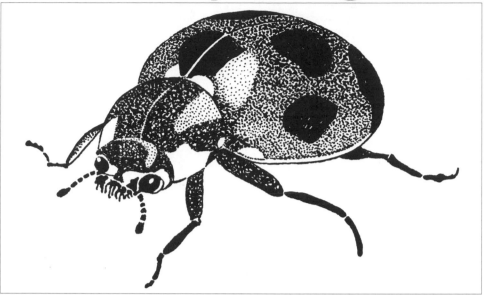

INTRODUCTION

Ladybugs are one of the more recognizable and popular insects that you can choose to have your children explore through a mini-habitat project. You can find these little red/orange and black ladybird beetles outside or order them from a nature supply company. They will undoubtedly provide a great deal of learning for all who observe their life cycle.

You can begin observing the growth and development of these aphid-eating beetles at any stage. They can reveal their entire life cycle within a month's time and provide your children with a close-at-hand view of the process. These insects hatch from eggs to larvae, change color, shed their skeleton by molting three times, and then undergo a metamorphosis to flying beetle.

CREATING THE ENVIRONMENT

Start by taking some time without the children to investigate your closest outside area for ladybugs or ladybug eggs. The books referenced in this section can help identify egg and larvae stages. If the beetles cannot be found, buy the eggs through a nature supply company.

To create the ladybug mini-habitat, you will need:

Container
A clear-sided, plastic shoe box will be a large enough habitat setting for 30 to 40 ladybugs. Keep top ventilated!

Food Source
Ladybugs eat small aphid insects (investigate for local source). Yeast food is available with commercially purchased insects for start-up. Small branches with tasty aphids will give the children a good view of the natural behavior of their ladybugs. Keep the leaves in a little water in a jar lid.

Reference Materials
The only other additions to your indoor habitat are recommended to enhance your children's discovery. Magnifiers, books and music on insects, including ladybug puppets. You can find ladybug puppets in the resource catalogs we have listed at the end of the chapter, children's educational supply stores, bookstores, and sometimes at teacher's conferences.

Suggestions for facilitating the ladybug mini-habitat:

1. Bring ladybugs out of their box at different stages for a closer look with magnifiers. Have the nonfiction reference books available to help children with recognition skills.

As children explore the ladybugs, take photos and make a poster with them. Use the children's words as captions for the pictures.

2. Carry the learning from the indoors to the out-of-doors by bringing the portable habitat outside. Either study them on a table outside for additional recall, or set some of them free to help make the connections of insects to plant life.

Provide art materials for children while outside with the ladybugs. You will get wonderful drawings and words to help in recalling the ladybugs later.

3. Encourage dramatic play inside and outside by making puppets. Music and song can start with a simple parody on a familiar tune using ladybugs and insects as the theme.

4. Field trips are a natural for insect discovery. Start in the yard, then venture to the neighborhood. Explore a city arboretum or nature center on a longer excursion.

Reference Books

Ladybug by Emery Bernhard, Holiday House, 1992.

Ladybug by Barrie Watts, Stopwatch Series, Silver Burdett Company, 1987.

Ladybugs by Sylvia Johnson, Lerner Publications, 1983.

Looking at Insects by David Suzuki, Warner Books, 1986.

The Ladybug and other Insects, a First Discover Book, Scholastic, Inc., 1989

Peterson First Guides—Insects by Christopher Leahy, Houghton Mifflin Company, 1987.

Resources

Insect Lore Products
P.O. Box 1535
Shafter, CA 93263
(805 746-6047)
(800 Live Bug)

BioQuip
17803 La Salle Avenue
Gardena, CA 90248
(310 324-0620)
(310 324-7931) FAX

Acorn Naturalists
17300 East 17th Street #J-236
Tustin, CA 92680
(800-422-8886)
(800-452-2802) Fax

Silver Burdett Press (Stopwatch Series)
P.O. Box 2649
Columbus, OH 43216
(800-848-9500)

Stories

The Grouchy Ladybug by Eric Carle, Crowell, 1977.

Poems

"Ladybug" by Joan Walsh Anglund, from *The Random House Book of Poetry For Children,* selected by Jack Prelutsky, Random House, 1983.

"Ladybug" from *Bugs: Poems,* by Mary Ann Hoberman, Viking, 1976.

Fish and Pond Environments

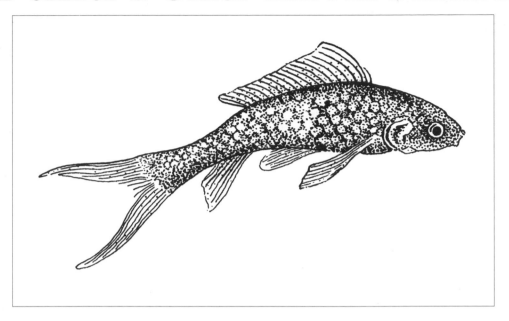

INTRODUCTION

We all remember fish in fishbowls from our own early childhood experiences. To enhance the more sterile environment of the traditional fishbowl, include living plants. Add a variety of fish and other water animals that can live in the same environment. The goal of this fish habitat is not to present a crystal clear bowl for decor but to achieve a balanced simulated pond environment.

If your community provides access (legal and convenient) to a natural pond setting, you may be able to take a few pond plants (from the roots with mud attached) and a good amount of pond water with algae and fish included. The pond water will be filled with organisms that will enhance the activity in the environment and your children's interest in it. Adding to your environment or creating it from scratch from an aquarium store can provide just as stimulating aquatic education for young children.

The intent of this project is to bring into focus the association of aquatic plants (including algae) and aquatic animals like fish and water snails. A totally balanced and self-sustaining environment is unlikely, so feeding fish and caretaking of the tank allows children to participate in keeping the tank inhabitants healthy. Bring the children into the process of building the environment and making additions and changes. You will see their interest, questions, and learning flourish.

CREATING THE ENVIRONMENT

You can acquire fish, aquatic snails, and plants from ponds or commercial aquarium stores. Maintain the water environment by regularly renewing it with pond water or find out what chemical balance your aquarium recommends. A simple additive may be required to offset toxic effects of chemicals in city drinking water.

To create the fish and pond mini-habitat, you will need:

Container
The physical environment can be a stationary glass aquarium or a portable plastic tank. Ask the children to help set up the environment. Lay mud or sand on the bottom of the tank and replant the pond (or aquarium) plants while you fill the tank until it is half full. Then add more water. When the sediment settles, add the fish and other animals. It is best if the animals get used to the temperature in the tank by floating in a closed plastic bag with water from the original environment for at least 30 minutes. Keep a net handy.

Food
Food for many of the animals will come from the naturally forming algae and the microorganisms that come in the pond water. Renew the algae

regularly. You may need to add a food supplement. If using aquarium store set-up, use recommended food.

Reference Material

Reference books on pond life and fish (see suggested titles), literature using pond settings, magazine photos or posters with enlarged pictures of pond environments, hand held magnifiers, a microscope if available, small plastic petri dish, large tweezers.

Suggestions for facilitating the fish and pond mini-habitat:

1. After you have checked on where your pond environment will originate (natural setting or aquarium), design a field trip to involve your children in the mini-habitat from the beginning. When creating the first stage of this habitat, don't crowd too much into the tank. Allow your children a clear view of their subjects with only a few plants and maybe a rock for a little mystery. As the children become familiar with the inhabitants, add new plants and animals.

2. Whether you add plants or animals as you go or stay with your originals, one of your fish will probably die. Your children will notice the missing part of the habitat, so don't try to hide the fact. A great deal more can be learned by allowing children to discover the dead animal and discuss how this is part of its life cycle. Take children's suggestions and try to direct the discussion toward putting the animal in the earth to help the plants grow. This experience will help them recognize how fish can help the plants grow to live much longer than fish or even the pond habitat.

3. A microscope provides a wonderful tool for a single or ongoing activity. As the children view all the action going on in a drop of pond water, their interest will be re-energized. They will get a chance to see the tiniest creatures that help the fish and other animals live. Compare the pond water with purified water for contrast. If a microscope is not available, use large magnifiers to provide an important closer look. Tweezers are helpful to move plants around in small plastic dishes.

Reference Books

Fish by Steve Parker, Alfred A. Knopf, 1990.

Fishes by Rosamund Kidman Cox, Usborne Publishing Limited, 1992.

Pond and River by Steve Parker, Alfred A. Knopf, 1988.

Underwater Alphabet Book by Jerry Palotta, Charlesbridge Publishing, 1991.

Peterson First Guide to Fishes by Lawrence M. Page, Houghton Mifflin Company, 1991.

Resources

Insect Lore Products
P.0. Box 1535
Shafter, CA 93263
(805 746-6047)
(800 Live Bug)

BioQuip
17803 La Salle Avenue
Gardena, CA 90248
(310 324-0620)
(310 324-7931) FAX

Acorn Naturalists
17300 East 17th Street #J-236
Tustin, CA 92680
(800-422-8886)
(800-452-2802) Fax

Resources Continued

Silver Burdett Press (Stopwatch Series)
P.O. Box 2649
Columbus, OH 43216
(800-848-9500)

Stories

Fish Eyes by Lois Ehlert, Harcourt Brace Jovanovich, 1990.

Fish Is Fish by Leo Lionni, Pantheon, 1970.

The Stream by Naomi Russell, E.P. Dutton, 1989.

Swimmy by Leo Lionni, Pantheon, 1963.

Poems

"Fish" by Arthur S. Bourinot, from Read-Aloud Rhymes for the Very Young, selected by Jack Prelutsky, Knopf, 1986.

"Fish" by Jack Prelutsky, from The Poetry Troupe: An Anthology of Poems to Read Aloud, compiled by Isabel Wilner, Scribner, 1977.

"Fish" by Mary Ann Hoberman, from Read-Aloud Rhymes for the Very Young, selected by Jack Prelutsky, Knopf, 1986.

Teacher Resources

Teacher Resources

ORGANIZATIONS

The National Audubon Society
950 Third Avenue
New York, NY 10022
(212 832-3200)

The Audubon Society is the most useful resource for teachers and parents of young children. Check your phone book for the number of a local Audubon group or call the national headquarters to find the group nearest you. In addition, some states have their own Audubon Societies, independent of the national organization, and are most likely to provide nature education programs for three- to five-year-olds. A few states have nature nursery schools that run three days a week during the school year. There are also Audubon summer camps for young children.

Nature Centers

Local nature centers or sanctuaries sponsored by Audubon groups often include exhibits specifically for young children in which they are encouraged to touch, explore, and ask questions. Most centers have guided nature trails and a staff prepared to talk with children about what they see. Almost always, staff members are knowledgable about local plants, animals, and geology. In some centers, the staff is trained in child development and nature. Some centers offer programs on weekends for families.

Curriculum Materials

"Reaching for Connections," Vols. 1 and 2, by David W. Stokes. Preschool-Grade 6; $5.50 each. A teacher's handbook of ideas for enhancing classroom programs and field trips. Order from Schlitz Audubon Center, 1111 East Brown Deer Road, Milwaukee, WI 53217; (414 352-2880).

Posters

"Birds of North America," "Rivers of Life," and others. Order from Northeast Audubon Center, Route 4, Box 171, Sharon, CT 06069 (203 364-0520).

Teacher Training

Several programs are available for teachers, including four-day sessions, programs aimed at inner-city classrooms, and a two-year Master of Science degree in Environmental Education. For information, contact the National Audubon Society at the address above.

National Wildlife Federation
1400 16th Street N.W.
Washington, DC 20036
(202 797-6800)

Currently, the best nature periodical for an early childhood classroom is the National Wildlife Federation magazine *Your Big Backyard*. A 20-page, monthly publication for two- to five-year-olds, *Your Big Backyard* includes beautiful photographs, stories, and nature information on a young child's level. Topics include: habitats, animal behavior during different seasons, animal babies, animal locomotion, and animal camouflage. Classroom children can enjoy *Your Big Backyard* independently or with their teachers.

The National Wildlife Federation also publishes *Nature Scope,* a magazine addressing specific science topics from the perspective of teachers and other adults who work with children. It is most useful for teachers of elementary-age children, but it also offers information and activities about animals and insects that are useful for teachers of three- and four-year-olds.

The National Wildlife Federation offers a variety of adult outdoor study programs ranging from three day Naturequests to one-week seminars.

Young Entomologists' Society (Y.E.S.)
1915 Peggy Place
Lansing MI 48910
(517 887-0499)

The Young Entomologists' Society is the most enthusiastic and comprehensive insect education group we have found. They publish a variety of periodicals, including the bimonthly *Insect World*. Although designed for older children, the magazine is useful for three- to five-year-olds. It contains insect facts, stories, poems, project ideas, instruction, and an activity page you can reproduce for the classroom.

Y.E.S. also publishes *Six-Legged Science: Insects in the Classroom*, a complete manual for teaching about insects to children of all ages; *Buggy Books: A Guide to Juvenile and Popular Books on Insects and Their Relations*, a listing of information on 736 books about insects. The Y.E.S. catalog is a comprehensive description of all their publications and other useful materials for keeping and observing insects.

RECOMMENDED BOOKS

Science

Ten Minute Field Trips: A Teacher's Guide to Using the School Ground for Environmental Studies, Second Edition, by Helen Ross Russell, National Science Teachers Association, 1990, 163 pages, $14.75.

Ten Minute Field Trips is an immediately satisfying and excellent book that simultaneously teaches the teacher or parent a tremendous amount about the natural world while showing us how to share our discoveries with children. Helen Russell helps teachers see the extensive possibilities of teaching about nature by using just what is at hand in both urban and rural settings.

Russell devotes part of the book to field trips on "hard-topped school grounds." What sort of nature study can you do if you are in the middle of the city with concrete surrounding your school? Russell answers: Study shadows, rock outcroppings, moss growing in sidewalk cracks, pigeons, sparrows, ants, wind, pollution, and more. What kind of mini-habitat is your local park? Russell explores the drama of life you might see there with children. (For example, if you find a pile of acorns that are half-eaten, it was most likely left by a squirrel who was keeping a lookout while he ate.)

Russell's ideas for teachers are thought provoking, yet are realistic and not complicated. Following the description of each subject, she includes ideas for classroom activities and guidance on teacher preparation and field trip possibilities.

Nature Activities for Early Childhood by Janet Nickelsburg, Addison-Wesley Publishing Company, 1976, 155 pages, $15.00.

We endorse the premise of this book: "to encourage children to make their own discoveries . . . that adults are partners as they present projects, and that the projects are meant to stimulate the child to stop, look and listen rather than to accomplish specific learning objectives." In addition, this straightforward book is compiled for the busy teacher, and has many useful and simple nature projects for children. Janet Nickelsburg endorses the use of children's own collections of feathers, rocks, leaves, or pebbles and a classroom nature center that displays the children's efforts. "Nature experiences presented to young children are not intended to be stepping stones to scientific concepts," she writes. "They are meant to be enjoyed for their own sake."

This book offers many appropriate activities for young children including outdoor group projects and projects using a small vocabulary. The chapters about animals and insects describe how to find, feed, and care for animals in the classroom. There is also an extensive and useful bibliography for children and adults at the end of each section.

Unlike *Ten Minute Field Trips*, this book does not take into account the teacher in the city surrounded by concrete, nor does it emphasize the interrelationships of all living things or recommend that children return the insects and animals to their natural habitat.

Early Childhood and Science by Margaret McIntyre, National Science Teachers Association, 136 pages, about 75 articles, $7.50.

This book is a compilation of articles that appeared in *Science and Children,* a monthly journal of the National Science Teachers Association. The articles demonstrate successful teaching experiences and are only a few pages long. Most were written by Margaret McIntyre. They are well written, and look at nature study as part of a science curriculum in which children are encouraged to explore materials, play with sand and water, and problem solve with one another.

The reader sees how science can lead children to write poetry or experience art, such as making rubbings of natural materials, all experiences that reinforce early science experiences. For example, in "A Living Science Laboratory," McIntyre describes a week-by-week, hands-on curriculum for teachers using the outdoors immediately outside the classroom. The session includes: plant exploration ("walk around the school to see how many different kinds of plants the children can locate. Naming is not necessary. Just keen observation of all growing plants."), weather exploration, tree walks, and insect finding.

The City Kid's Field Guide by Ethan Heberman, Simon and Schuster with WGBH-Boston, 1989, 50 pages, $14.95.

This book, like *Ten Minute Field Trips,* is especially useful for city teachers who are looking for nature experiences for young children. The author has taken any North American city and turned it into a nature laboratory for young children. *City Kid's Field Guide* is filled with vignettes about common creatures we find around us and their relationships to one another and to us. It explains why you would want a praying mantis in your garden or a house spider and centipede in your house. It explains what it is like to be a housefly and why it always escapes when swatted by a human. This book is colorful in its presentation and amusing for teachers who want to share their growing knowledge of plant and animal life in houses, parks, window ledges, and vacant lots.

Northeast Field Guide to Environmental Education edited by Sue Hale and Jeff Schwartz, Antioch New England Graduate School, 1991, 470 pages, $26.00.

If you live in the Northeastern United States and want to take a group of children out to a wildlife refuge or a nature center, you are in luck. This book is an up-to-date, complete guide to every possible museum, planetarium, national forest, state park, and arboretum. For each site, this book lists the address, phone number, director's name, type of programs offered, age range for whom the programs are appropriate, size of the site, whether there are internships (should you want to be trained there), and what sort of resources or materials are offered. This is a wonderful guide to environmental education for this part of the country.

Early Childhood and Teaching

Developmentally Appropriate Practice in Early Childhood Programs Serving Children from Birth Through Age 8 by S. Bredekamp, National Association for the Education of Young Children, 1987.

Issues in Curriculum: What Resources Do Preschool Teachers Need? by E. Jones, Pacific Oaks Occasional Papers, 1989.

The Play's the Thing: Teachers' Roles in Children's Play by E. Jones and G. Reynolds, Teachers College Press, 1992.

Engaging Children's Minds: The Project Approach by Lilian Katz and S. Chard, Ablex, 1989.

Environmental Education at the Early Childhood Level, Ruth Wilson, Editor, North American Association for Environmental Education, 1994.

Children and Community Violence

Children in Danger: Coping with the Consequences of Community Violence by James Garbarino, et al., Jossey-Bass, 1991.

Children and Death

The Tenth Good Thing about Barney by Judith Viorst, Macmillan Publishing, 1988.

Lifetimes: The Beautiful Way to Explain Death to Children by Bryan Mellonie and Robert Ingpen, Bantam Books, 1983.

RECOMMENDED ARTICLES

"The Gift of a Butterfly" by Kathryn A. Hofschild, *Young Children,* March 1991.

This article describes what happens in one classroom when a painted lady butterfly emerges from its chrysalis unable to fly, and then the reaction of the children and teacher when the butterfly dies. The article is a marvelous example of what can happen when the teacher is able to share her own feelings. The article asks: What sort of emotional attachment is made by the teacher and the children as they take special care of a creature? How can you expand this to include further understanding of other animals or people with disabilities?

"Plant a Potato—Learn about Life (and Death)" by Edna Furman, *Young Children,* November 1990.

This article tells the down-to-earth story of a teacher and a class of parents and toddlers. The class roots sweet potatoes, plants a garden, and grows simple things from the supermarket. The manner in which this teacher shares her enthusiasm and respect for the life cycle with the parents and children makes this an important article. The author gives the reader a valuable lesson about nature instruction in which the teacher is not an expert—she did not anticipate the complications that arose as some things lived and many died. Instead, the teacher is calm, direct, and respectful of parents, children, and the rhythm of living things.

"All about Ants: Discovery Learning in the Primary Grades" by Amelia Klein, *Young Children,* July 1991.

The ant study described in this article could be used most fully by teachers of elementary age children, but the premise is applicable for teachers of younger children. What can teachers do if they find children smashing ants on the playground? This teacher began by preaching to the children about the beauty of all living things and then sees that the children learned nothing from her speech. She realized that she needed to offer them a cognitive experience to arouse their curiosity. She asked them what they would like to know about ants, and the children compiled a list, including: What do ants eat? Why do they go into the anthill? Do ants sleep? Where do ants go when it rains? The article would be helpful to teachers who discover a similar interaction and would like to turn the situation from a massacre into a nature study.

Special Opportunities in Nature Education Training

The Roger Tory Peterson Institute of Natural History
311 Curtis Street
Jamestown, New York 14701
716-665-2473

The Roger Tory Peterson Institute is a national not-for-profit educational organization that is dedicated to promoting nature education. It conducts staff development workshops for teachers at major nature centers, zoos, museums, and school districts throughout the country. Membership benefits include *Peterson Field Guides* and *Birds, Bats, and Butterflies,* a quarterly leaflet that provides practical and inexpensive ideas that help parents of young children share wholesome experiences in nature.

Naturkind Teacher Training

The Roger Tory Peterson Institute of Natural History's Naturkind Training Program provides workshops specifically to help teachers implement *Snail Trails and Tadpole Tails.* Offered at sites throughout the country, the Naturkind workshop provides early childhood teachers with an opportunity to:

- practice techniques to develop observation skills and to identify plants and animals;

- become acquainted with specific aninals in mini habitats, reference books, and other suggested classroom materials; and

- meet teachers who have successfully used the materials with their classes

Participants receive all start-up materials so they can implement the program in their classroom the following day if they wish. For information contact:

> The Education Department
> The Roger Tory Peterson Institute of Natural History
> 311 Curtis Street
> Jamestown, NY 14701
> Phone: 716-665-2473   FAX: 716-665-3794

Other Redleaf Press Publications

All the Colors We Are: The Story of How We Get Our Skin Color — Outstanding full-color photographs show the beautiful diversity of human skin color. The simple text offers children an accurate explanation.

Basic Guide to Family Child Care Record Keeping : Fourth Edition — Clear instructions on keeping necessary family day care business records.

Business Receipt Book — Receipts specifically for family child care payments improve your record keeping; 50 sets per book.

Busy Fingers, Growing Minds — Over 200 original and traditional finger plays, with enriching activities for all parts of a curriculum.

Calendar-Keeper — Activities, family day care record keeping, recipes and more. Updated annually. Most popular publication in the field.

Child Care Resource & Referral Counselors & Trainers Manual — Both a ready reference for the busy phone counselor and a training guide for resource and referral agencies.

Developing Roots & Wings: A Trainer's Guide to Affirming Culture In Early Childhood Programs — The training guide for Root & Wings, with 11 complete sessions and over 170 training activities.

The Dynamic Infant — Combines an overview of child development with innovative movement and sensory experiences for infants and toddlers.

Enrolllment/Medical Form — Information required by most states, from health history to emergency parental consent.

Family Child Care Contracts and Policies — Samples contracts and policies, and how - to information on using them effectively to improve tour business.

Family Child Care Tax Workbook — Updated every year, latest step-by-step information on forms, depreciation, etc.

Heart to Heart Caregiving: A Sourcebook of Family Day Care Activities, Projects and Practical Provider Support — Excellent ideas and guidance written by an experienced provider.

Kids Encyclopedia of Things to Make and Do — Nearly 2,000 art and craft projects for children aged 4-10.

The (No Leftovers!) Child Care Cookbook — Over 80 child-tested recipes and 20 menus suitable for family child care providers and center programs. CACFP creditable.

Parent/Provider Policies — Easy-to-use, 2-part carbonless form that helps you create a thorough, professional parent agreement.

Pathways to Play — Help children improve their play skills with a skill checklist and planned activities.

Practical Solutions to Practically Every Problem: The Early Childhood Teacher's Manual — Over 300 proven developmentally appropriate solutions for all kinds of classroom problems.

Roots & Wings: Affirming Culture in Early Childhood Programs — A new approach to multicultural education that helps shape positive attitudes toward cultural differences.

Sharing in the Caring — Packet to help establish good relationships between providers and parents with agreement forms and other information.

Those Mean Nasty Dirty Downright Disgusting but… Invisible Germs — A delightful story that reinforces for children the benefits of frequent hand washing.

Transition Magician: Strategies for Guiding Young Children in Early Childhood Programs — Turn difficult, boring, transition times into magical moments for children!

Call for Catalog or Ordering Information 1-800-423-8309